D1624366

Single Parents in Black America

A Study in Culture and Legitimacy

A Study in Culture and Legitimacy

Annie S. Barnes

Wyndham Hall Press

SINGLE PARENTS IN BLACK AMERICA
A Study in Culture and Legitimacy

by

Annie S. Barnes

Library of Congress
Catalog Card Number
87-051006

ISBN 1-55605-024-0 (paperback)
ISBN 1-55605-023-2 (hardback)

Dedicated to my Husband, Daughter and Geraldine

BLACK SINGLE COMMUNITY MOTHERS AND FATHERS

CONTENTS

TABLES

PROLOGUE

For several decades social scientists have written about single parenthood among blacks. They have studied its frequency, household structure, poverty, absence of fathers, and intergenerational perpetuation, yet the studies do not show the history of single parents' life through their own eyes and even fewer studies focus on fathers' and mothers' feelings about parenthood and their significant relationships. Also, the studies delineate only a few causes and solutions, and as far as I can determine, attention has not been paid to what single mothers and fathers would do if they could start their lives over. Because of my concern with these issues as well as with those that had been studied, students in my Family course, my student assistants, and I have researched single parenthood off and on over the last fifteen years and conducted a total of seven single parenthood studies. Five are included in this volume and two additional studies, about college, single fathers and college, single mothers, comprise two other books on black, single parenthood.

The single parents in this book describe the world they live in and what they made of it. According to Banks, "... the way people make sense of their lives, the web of meaning and identity they weave for themselves, has a significance and importance of its own" (1980:xxv). Banks captures the underlying reason for asking our single parent respondents to describe their own lives. The portraits and descriptions in these chapters -- from questionnaire, interview, participant observation, and oral history data -- describe both their memory of the history of single parenthood in their own lives as well as the way they now experience it.

The aims in this book are to utilize five studies to describe single parenthood, analyze the findings, test Bronislaw Malinowski's Principle of Legitimacy, relate the findings to Oscar Lewis' Culture of Poverty model, suggest addenda to this model, and abstract a self-correcting poverty model and four pregnancy prevention models. Additionally, the findings are used to suggest single parenthood hypotheses for further research.

These goals were achieved by asking some specific questions about single parenthood. One set of questions concerns the background of the respondents. The questions asked about their background were: How early did the respondents experience sex? Where did their first sex experiences occur? Why sex participation? Why pregnancy? What were the birthing stages? Did the respondents become parents more than once? What were the respondents' survival strategies? In retrospect, what would the respondent do, if they could relive their lives with their present experience? Another set of questions deals with their relationships. We asked: What are the respondents' relationship with the mothers or fathers of their children? What is their relationship with their children? What is their relationship with their mothers? What is their relationship with the mothers of the men who fathered their children? Still other questions used the findings in the five studies to determine answers to other central questions in the literature. The questions included: Is Malinowski's Principle of Legitimacy supported in Norfolk and Tidewater, Virginia? Do the findings in our studies support the Culture of Poverty model? Do the findings in our study modify the Culture of Poverty model? Is there self-correcting poverty coexisting with self-perpetuating poverty? What are the solutions to single parenthood? Also, we used the findings to determine whether single fathers have an advantage over single mothers? The final questions helped develop models. Hence, four models are suggested for pregnancy prevention. They are Youth Advocates for Singlehood Without Parenthood Model, Human Sexuality Training in Schools: Seventh through Twelfth Grade Model, Parental Agenda for Childrearing Model, and Home Sex Education: Fatherhood Prevention Model. Concerned with single parenthood in the context of interpersonal relations, this Prologue to our studies is begun with the oral history of Karma Renford, pseudonym for one of the 161 respondents described in this book.

Karma Renford

Headnotes

Karma, a twenty-seven year old single mother of two children, has over two years of college education and works as an index clerk, for $700.00 a month, in Norfolk, Virginia. According to Karma, she is overqualified for the position as well as overworked and underpaid. Because she has three mouths to feed, as she noted, she needs to work, though she lives with her mother. Karma was thirteen years old when she had her first sex experience and her boyfriend was fourteen. During a telephone conversation, he convinced her to have sex. A short time later, Karma went to his mother's house. While the young man's mother remained upstairs, she and her boyfriend engaged in sex downstairs. It was six years later before she had her next sex experience and soon became pregnant. Before pregnancy, Karma's father had not told her anything about boys and sex, but her mother had explained its disadvantages; however, she does not recall being introduced to birth control. Karma begins by talking about relations with her mother. I remember that my relationship with my mother was not open. Because I didn't respond very much, our conversations were one sided. I was a rejecting kid. When I had my first child, I was nineteen years old and away from home. If I had been living at home with Mama, I probably would not have a child, or if I had gotten pregnant, I probably would have gotten an abortion. I think mothers should encourage abortions because early responsibility as a mother keeps a girl from enjoying life. In my opinion, black mothers don't try to cover up for their daughters by encouraging abortions; instead, they say, "If you make your bed hard, lay in it."

Upon learning that I was pregnant, though we were not using birth control, I was shocked. I neither knew what to do or where to go. It is a lonely feeling when one has neither a source of advice nor a friend for friendship. I knew she would reject me because she stressed school, education, and fun. When I became pregnant, Mama felt that something was wrong; therefore, she came to Washington, D.C. where I was living.

However, I wanted the first baby, but my boyfriend had not made such request. Rather than get an abortion, I had the baby to spite Mama and demonstrate concern for my boyfriend. As I mentioned earlier, my mother had told me the advantages of preventing motherhood. I took a negative view toward what she told me, but now I wish I had listened. My life would have been much better and I could have achieved a college degree in computer programming.

Because the children were like toys, at first, motherhood was fun. That is, I played with them, cuddled them, pampered

iii

them, and thought the sun rose and set in them. However, soon the price tag went up; that is, they gave me something to think about. They have so many kinds of attitudes until I don't know what to do. Single motherhood becomes more hectic as they get older. It is hard to cater to the needs of both. I discipline them and will not give them too much freedom in junior high school. I tell them now, when you get a job and take care of me, you can tell me what to do. If you raise your hand, you will get the results. I cut down on their freedom or time for play. I take away from them things they enjoy most. They like to ride bicycles; instead, when they misbehave, sometimes I lock them in the closet for ten to fifteen minutes. By the time they come out, they have calmed down. When I whip them, I hit myself more than I hit them.

When I learned that I was expecting my second child, I was frightened. The second one disturbed me most -- because I had just accepted the fact of one child. After the birth of the second child, I thought, if my boyfriend leaves, how will I support our two children? What happened is that he left us before the baby was a year old. Life got harder. I found myself in a great big world with two kids and not knowing how to take care of them. I always had someone to take care of me, but now I must take care of somebody. How? I asked myself. To go through the experience of single, parenthood, I needed a support system. Therefore, I was fortunate to find a boyfriend who gives me financial support. He is unmarried -- the way he must be -- for I am not out for sharing anything, especially my man. I cannot affort to be neglected. He visits often, is loving, and gives me moral and economic support.

Before I began expecting my children, their father and I never discussed how they would be supported, but this is something that all couples should decide beforehand. I support my children, as much as I can, by working every day and obtaining assistance from my boyfriend and the welfare department.

Welfare life is a difficult experience. The welfare department makes one go through many changes. Because they utilize a slow procedure locating fathers of our children, though we usually know their location, we often do not report them. To do so, delays paychecks while the department does the paper work and locates them. If they curtailed the red tape, mothers would report the location of the fathers of their children. Besides, the public assistance department asks one's life history and charges a small fee, based on the mother's income, to file papers for child support. Then they go through the process of locating and telling the man he's a father. Often this process is followed by father denial, petition of mother, and blood tests. Once it is proven that he is the father of a woman's child, the judge figures out, on the basis of the father's income, how much child support to require. Further, the welfare department does not deliver services correctly -- they treat us like animals.

When I had my children, government assistance was not considered. I don't want it; I prefer a good job that I work on every day. When you work, you don't have to report to anyone. A job gives me a sense of dignity, self respect; I am not a statistic. Welfare is okay for a while for people who can't do better; and makes it convenient to become a single parent; the more babies, the longer women can stay home and let taxpayers pay. I would rather pay for my own children.

Beside economic difficulties, I also have another serious problem. My children's father only gives them gifts at Christmas and Easter and $50.00 each per year; and he is not loving toward them. However, my greatest difficulty is that both children often say, "Mama, I want a Daddy," but I can't go to the grocery store and buy one.

Another problem is that I attempt to use my children's love as a substitute for their father's love, but I am still empty. Because he is married, now I don't love him. The feeling has gone -- I have no type of physical feeling for him. Of course, when I was carrying his children, though at first, I was disappointed, cold, and blunt with the second child, I loved him more than before because I was carrying something that was part of us. I could not love it without loving him. Moreover, earlier his family treated me like I was a family member, but now we do not communicate. On the other hand, Mama was cold in the beginning, but now we have a better relationship. We are more open and discuss my problems. Yet, it is not all a mother-daughter relationship should be because I disobeyed.

This experience has taught me that, if one has a chance to better herself, she should move on. As long as you help yourself, someone will help you. If you find the achievement you desire, let nobody distract your thoughts from its accomplishment.

In conclusion, if I could live my life over and know what I have experienced, it would be a whole lot different. I would finish college and have only one child after marriage. After I became pregnant, life is the way I thought it would be. I thought it would be h..., hard work, determination, problems, trials, and tribulation. Maybe one day I will get lucky, find a nice man, and get married. In the beginning, I was in this great big world with a family, with no job, with nobody to help. However, I couldn't let it get the best of me -- I could not give up. It made me beware of people. People -- lovers and friends, are not what they say they are. I have learned that one can't depend on anybody but herself. Men will get all they can from women, but the h... with us.

My advice to young girls is that, if you can do anything to keep from having a baby, outside marriage, please do so. Go to school, get an education, see that you can take care of yourself. Too many children, without food, housing, and clothing are a problem. Young girls, stop, look, and listen! Young girls, stop and talk with your mothers and fathers rather than with other people! Ask yourself the question: Do I want my children brought up on welfare? Is the man willing to stick by me? And the answer to the last question is, you don't know. Young girls, you must be self-sufficient in your own right. And I highly recommend constant use of birth control.

Setting the tone for this work, Karma indicates that pregnancy and motherhood are complex problems with complex causes and results requiring multiple solutions.

My gratitude is boundless to Karma, the lone respondent from Diggs Park, a Norfolk, Virginia housing development, to Maria, the respondent who taught this study the sex power concept and the lone respondent from still another housing development in Norfolk, Virginia, and to the 160 other single fathers and mothers who shared generously about the nature of single parenthood. Without their warmth and generosity, this book could not have been written. For their cooperation in making known the reality of single parenthood, I hope their children will benefit not only from their enhanced awareness of what can cause and possibly prevent single parenthood, but also from the findings in their experience that I hope will serve as the impetus for programs to combat single parenthood.

I am grateful to Gerald L. Davis, James A. Nolan, and Frederick C. Gamst, who offered helpful comments on a previous version of Chapter Four.

To Ingrid E. Legion, Director of Norfolk Pregnancy Hotline, thanks for supplying unwed birth statistics for Norfolk and Virginia. Thanks to Denita Square, Jeanne Clarke, and Shelcie Moss, Norfolk State University Students and my research assistants, who contributed to data collection. Again, I happily acknowledge my appreciation to the single parent-respondents in Norfolk and Tidewater, Virginia for a warm and in-depth research experience that made this book possible.

Annie S. Barnes
School of Social Science
Norfolk State University
Norfolk, Virginia 23504

CHAPTER ONE

INTRODUCTION

This book is about urban, black, single mothers and fathers in two low rent housing developments -- Young Park and Calvert Park -- in Norfolk, Virginia, and single mothers in Tidewater, Virginia. In my research among blacks since 1969, I have used the family as a unit of study and varied approaches to family life. In The Black Middle Class Family, I described a wide spectrum of black middle class family behavior: residential patterns, voluntary associations, neighborhood behavior, the home and its environs, family and food ritual, and family relations. In Black Women: Interpersonal Relationships in Profile, I discussed interpersonal relations with the respondents and their employers, their husbands, and their female friends and acquaintances.

In this book, one aim is to describe relationships important to black single mothers and fathers through their own eyes and what they would do, if they could start life over. Also, this work seeks to test Malinowski's Principle of Legitimacy, relate the Culture of Poverty model to our findings about urban, poor, black, single parent families, determine whether the model needs to be broadened, and ascertain whether the data indicate a self-correcting poverty model and pregnancy prevention models. Because of the longitudinal nature of our fieldwork on single parents, use of the oral history method, supplemented by interview and observation data, and the similarity in the questions asked in each study as well as new questions not asked in previous studies, we are able to provide a data based assessment of the poverty model, the self-perpetuating poverty corollary, the legitimacy principle, and other questions raised in this study.

Single Parenthood Among Blacks in the United States

Because this research is about single black fathers and mothers, first, we describe single parenthood in the United States.

1

It has been a frequent line of inquiry in family studies. As early as the mid forties, Drake and Cayton "found that between 1928 and 1933 about 24,000 Negro babies were born in Chicago; 2,000 of whom were born out of wedlock mainly of young, low-income mothers" (Drake and Cayton, 1945:589-590). In effect, Drake and Cayton's recognition of the disorganization of the black family in Chicago prefigured Frazier's explication in 1957. The steady rise in single parenthood, among blacks, led Moynihan to indicate, in the sixties, that births to single, black mothers were increasing at an alarming rate (Rainwater and Yancey 1967:8). Then, in the early seventies, Cox noted that "over half the children born out of wedlock are nonwhite although only 12 percent of the population are nonwhite" (1972:161), a trend that continued throughout the seventies. And by the beginning of the eighties, more than half of the black births were counted as products of single parentage.

According to the Culture of Poverty model and tangle of pathology, unwed births are a self-perpetuating trait among poor blacks. Hylan Lewis provided some evidence that unwed motherhood is perpetuated at least two generations; hence, he found in Kent that "Illegitimacy and delinquency occur in two generations in the same household" (1955:96). According to Clark, the boy who fathers an illegitimate child does not lose, "for where is he going? The path to any higher status seems closed to him in any case" (1965:72). Similarly, Hylan Lewis found in Kent that "Many men admit such facts and openly or tacitly recognize their issues; and there is a tendency among some men to boast about the number of children they have "out in the bushes" (Lewis 1955:88). And Hendricks noted that in a sample of adolescent fathers, 70 percent "saw nothing wrong in having a child out of wedlock" (1981:135).

Social scientists have also been concerned with the causes of single parenthood. For example, Frazier (1957:319), Lewis (1955:85), and Roebuck and McGee (1957:112) found it related to type of family organization. It also seems related to early male heterosexual involvement, for in a study of ten to seventeen year olds, unlike whites, it was seen that twelve and thirteen year old Negro boys were significantly more involved in such behavior as dating and going steady than Negro girls. Similarly, unwed parenthood appears related to early female sexual behavior. Hence, Schulz reported that "... many girls have had sexual relations by the time they enter high school. It is considered the normal thing to do to 'please' your boyfriend" (Schulz 1969:48). Single parenthood is also related to failure to use contraception; in this regard, Schulz (1969:53) reported that ignorance of effective contraception, fear of using it, and failure to plan ahead for sexual relations account for out of wedlock children. A related finding is that "Sexuality is not discussed in the homes. Most boys and girls discover sex with close friends, and the girls quite frequently with older sisters; as a result, there is little understanding about sexual matters despite great practical experience (Schulz 1969:46). However, it has been found that some adolescents understand sexual matters. For example, in a select sample of adolescent black fathers, Hendricks found that "70 percent of the adolescent fathers had sexual intercourse with the mothers of their first children with full knowledge of the potential outcome, that is, pregnancy" (Hendricks 1981:136).

Low self esteem has also been related to single fatherhood. For example, Clark notes that "The marginal young Negro male tends to identify his masculinity with the number of girls he attracts. The high incidence of illegitimacy among Negro young people reflects this pervasive fact" (Clark 1965:71). Clark also seems to suggest that female single parenthood results from low self esteem. Therefore, he states that "... a child is a symbol of the fact that she is a woman, and she may gain from having something of her own." It is apparent that some black males and females use single parenthood, rather than educational and work achievement, as a measure of success.

Another concern in the black, family literature is about motherhood twice or more. Though such concern has been raised in the context of the culture of poverty and tangle of pathology, few studies have been made. However, an interest in this topic has been shown; for example, Griswold et. al. included in their Contra Costa, California study some reference to single and multiple births. The forty black women in the sample were evenly divided between uniparae and multiparae women (1967:8); and social heredity nor an explanation based upon historical illegitimacy was supported (Griswold 1967:15,16). However, it was found that 60 percent of the uniparae and 69 percent of the multiparae had siblings with children born out of wedlock (Griswold 1967:16). Though there is not much difference between uniparae and multiparae, it is significant to find that such large percentages have single parent siblings. Hence, the National Council on Illegitimacy in New York City warns that "the effects of an illegitimate pregnancy on the younger children must be considered - particularly in terms of preventive education" (Garland 1967:37). It is apparent that another significant addition to the Culture of Poverty model is that not only is poverty, single parenthood in this case, intergenerationally transmitted, but it is also intragenerationally perpetuated.

There has been minimal attention to expectations in couple's relationships at the onset of pregnancy. According to Clark, "If when the girl becomes pregnant, the boy deserts or refuses to marry her, it is often because neither can sustain an intimate relationship; both seem incapable of the tenderness that continues beyond immediate gratification" (1965:73). Further, according to Clark, "The lower class girl does not expect to hold the boy. The marginal Negro female uses her sex instead, to gain personal affirmation. She is desired and that is almost enough" (1965:72). However, Schulz differs with Clark. Schulz notes that one of the positive aspects "of pregnancy out of wedlock is that it may be used in catching a husband. To intentionally become pregnant in order to get a husband presupposes the existence of norms that dictate a man's responsibility to care for what he has brought into the world" (1969:155). Similarly, Willie notes that "the illegitimate child is frequently a by-product of the woman's search for a husband. Viewed from this perspective, out-of-wedlock conceptions reflect not so much a breakdown in family structure as a broken promise" (1976:168). Willie adds that "All too frequently, he is the man who got away. In many cases, the woman misunderstands the paramour and miscalculates, with tragic results" (1976:168). These are important findings about expectations in expectant parents' relationships. Nonetheless, there is still a need for more agreement in the interpersonal aspirations of expectant and pre/expectant parents, which presupposes substantial data for drawing conclusions.

There has also been minimal attention to the relationship between single parents and between single fathers and their children. Hence, according to Hendricks, "There is a dearth of information on the unwed adolescent male partner of the teen or preteen woman who becomes pregnant. There is even less information on his attitude toward fatherhood and his relationship with the mother of his first child," especially black fathers (Hendricks 1981:131). Nevertheless, Hendricks found, in his study, that "the majority of the unwed adolescent fathers perceived their relationship with the mothers to be one of love" (1981:136). The serious problems they noted were child support, denial of the opportunity to see the child, lack of understanding, communication and disagreements (Hendricks 1981:136).

Even so, Clark reported that "The marginal young people in the ghetto, through their tentative and sporadic relationships, are seeking love, affection, and acceptance perhaps more desperately than young people elsewhere. Person-to-person relationships are, for many, a compensation for society's rejection" (1965:72). These findings also indicate the need for case studies, such as the ones in this work, to provide greater understanding of interpersonal relations between single parents and their feelings about parenthood and the opposite parent of their children.

Limited attention has also been paid to black mothers' support systems. According to Hill, one of the strengths of black families is that they are able to meet the needs of its members, including adoption of children born to single family members (1971:3). For example, "160,000 out of wedlock black babies were absorbed in 1969 by already existing black families. This absorption helps to minimize the number of new black families headed by single women" (Hill 1971:3). According to Hill, "this feat of self-help among black families is remarkable when one realizes their precarious economic position" (1971:7). Similarly, Martin and Martin noted that in two small towns in central Missouri and northern Florida and two urban areas, Cleveland and Kansas, City, that formal and informal adoption of relatives occurs, but "Children born out of wedlock are most often subject to informal adoption" (1978:42).

Black men also lend support to women with children. Schulz has noted that one type of supportive boyfriend among black women is supportive biological fathers. They assist women by helping "support the children that they have brought into the world without seriously considering marriage to one another" (Schulz 1970:236).

There has been concern about the attitude of black girls toward becoming mothers. Bernard sheds light on this question. She reported that it was "asked by Elizabeth Herzog of the Children's Bureau several years ago in a review of all the available research on the subject" (1960:50). Herzog found "for every study that reported a matter-of-fact acceptance, there was one that reported condemnation or another that reported both; for every study that reported shame or guilt in the part of the young mother, there was another that reported none" (1966:50). Similarly, "At a round-table discussion by Urban League community leaders in 1964, there was the same lack of agreement on what the facts were, let alone "the truth" (When one participant said that Negro society accepted out-of-wedlock births, there was loud denial from some of the others); it is "possible that both sets of observers might be right. It may be the presence of women from both cultures in populations of unmarried mothers that confounds research" (Bernard 1966:50).

There is additional evidence that black girls are not favorable toward bearing children out of wedlock. For example, in a hypothetical study of 100 Negro college girls and 100 Negro noncollege girls, "over three fifths stated that they would feel ashamed and embarrassed, if they become pregnant, and half of them defined guilt feelings in religious or moral terms; but only thirteen of the subjects related that they would feel exploited by the putative father" (Himes 1964:346); and in a comparative study by Haney et al. of black women who have illegitimate children and those who have legitimate children, it was found that the never marrieds desired a lower average number of children, and only a low proportion have a positive attitude toward pregnancy (1975:363-365). Himes also found in his hypothetical study of 100 Negro college and 100 Negro noncollege girls that they "anticipated rejection from the school while parents, siblings, and best friends were viewed as most accepting" (1964:345).

The Principle of Legitimacy

Using our five single parenthood studies, including a study of single fathers, we decided to test Malinowski's Principle of Legitimacy. According to this sociological law, "no child should be brought into the world without a man - and one man at that - assuming the role of sociological father..." (Malinowski 1966:35). Because of high rates of children born out of wedlock in the Caribbean, Goode states that "doubt has been raised as to whether a "sociological father" exists, and indeed various writers have spoken of a matrifocal family" (1960:22). Hence, according to Goode, Henriques comments (regarding Jamaica) that there is no moral sanction against "concubinage," Herskovits and Herskovits, assert that, in Trinidad, "there is no social disability imposed by the community because of legitimacy or illegitimacy," and Melville J. Herskovits, notes that among several classes of children, including those born outside mar- riage, children born out of wedlock in Haiti are not "at any special social disadvantage" (1960:23). Goode also notes that, according to Kreiselman, in Martinique, "The legitimate and illegitimate share the same status" and Stycos and Mintz note that, in Puerto Rico, "the rule of legitimacy fails" (Goode 1960:24).

Goode disagrees that the principle of legitimacy does not exist in the Carribean. Hence, he noted that "Malinowski was stating a proposition about a cultural element: he asserted that the norm would always be found, not that the members of the society would obey it under specified conditions" (1960:23). According to Goode, though at first glance, it appears that Malinowski's rule of legitimacy in the Caribbean is refuted, research reports "prove conclusively that the norm exists, since in fact marriage is the ideal, and those who violate the rule do suffer penalties" (1960:24). For example, according to Goode, in Jamaica, Edith Clark shows that priests may shame couples, Henriques noted "Both upper and middle class opinion is set against "concubinage," and Cohen indicates that "Few men (in Rocky Roads) allow their women to bring their illegitimate children into the union, if they do marry" (1960:24). In the same community, according to Cohen, illegitimate chil- dren are subjected to more physical rejection and pressures of sibling rivalry (Goode 1960:240. Similarly, based on findings in the work of Herskovits and Herskovits, Goode notes that in Trinidad couples marry after living together "for the position it gives the family" while from Herskovits' work, Goode notes that the church union is significant in Haiti (1960:25). In regard to Martinique, Goode reports that Bastien observed that "The consciousness of their social inferiority so troubles ... (them) ... that few resist the temptation to explain the cause of their situation ..." and Kreiselman adds that, "parents are angry at the pregnancy of the unmarried girl, who may have to leave home" (1960:25).

As a result, Goode concluded that though various observers have asserted that the principle does not exist in the Caribbean societies, "unequivocally, Malinowski's Principle of Legitimacy indeed exists in these societies. Birth out of wedlock is not a 'cultural alternative.' There is no special approval of the consensual union, no 'counter-norm' in favor of such a union" (1960:26). Further, Goode says, "For at least the Caribbean, where this explanation has been widespread, it has been shown that both mother and child have a lower status outside the legal union, that women prefer to be married, and there is general agreement that the ideal family relationship is that of marriage" (1961:911). However, Goode does suggest a reformulation of Malinowski's principle that takes into consideration the foundation of the principle which is status placement rather than locating a father as a 'protector' and differential norm commitment by social strata (1960:27).

Culture of Poverty Model

This research also focuses on another central question in the black, family literature -- the relevance of the Culture of Poverty model to black family life. Building on Frazier's community and family disorganization hypothesis, Oscar Lewis developed the Culture of Poverty model. Lewis viewed poverty and its associated traits as a "subculture with its own structure and rationale, as a way of life which is passed down from generation to generation along family lines" (1965:xliii). Also, Lewis noted that "it represents an effort to cope with feelings of hopelessness and despair which develop from the realization of the improbabilty of achieving success in terms of the value and goals of the larger society" (1965:xliv). Beside, Lewis noted that, "It is a culture in the traditional anthropological sense in that it provides human beings with a design for living, with a ready-made set of solutions for human problems, and so serves a significant adaptive function" (1966:19). The model identifies seventy traits of poverty found in four spheres of life: "the relationship between the subculture and larger society;

the nature of the slum community; the nature of the family; and the attitudes, values and character structure of the individual" (Lewis 1965:xlv). Lewis particularly noted similarities among the poor in family structure, "in interpersonal relations, in spending habits, in their value systems and their orientation in time" (1966:19). Furthermore, Lewis suggests that research should focus on the slum community and family rather than the individual and a distinction between poverty and the culture of poverty (1966:19).

The Sixties

Though Lewis propounded the Culture of Poverty model almost thirty years ago, it has received continuous attention over the decades. Starting in the sixties, Lewis, himself, noted the effects -- increased domestic expenditure through the Office of Economic Opportunity along with "parallel expansion of publication in the social sciences on the subject of poverty" (1966:19). When writing about poverty, social scientists were concerned with each poverty sphere described by Lewis. Hence, the poverty literature includes the relationship between the subculture and larger society. For example, social scientists noted such traits characterizing urban, poor, blacks, as education (Clark 1965:38; Rutledge and Gass 1968:98; Shulz 1969:71-78), unemployment, underemployment, low wages, and a chronic shortage of cash (Clark 1965:27-29, 34; Moynihan 1967:19-25; Liebow 1967:29-71; Hannerz 1969:179; Rainwater 1971:27). Similarly, social scientists described varied traits characterizing urban, poor, blacks on the local community level. They are substandard living quarters (Clark 1965:30-34; Hannerz 1969:179) and transient, neighbor and kin relations (Clark 1965:47-50; Liebow 1967:218; Moynihan 1967:5-14). Further, on the family level, social scientists noted that single parenthood characterizes urban, poor blacks (Clark 1965:27; Liebow 1967:54, 212) while on the individual level they noted drug and alcohol addition (Clark 1965:27), nonutilitarian expressive behavior (Hannerz 1969:59-69), and low self esteem (Schulz 1969:74-75). Hence, these findings support Lewis' observation that the poverty literature expanded considerably in the sixties. And equally important is that during the sixties social scientists found useful the four spheres of life identified in Oscar Lewis' Culture of Poverty model.

9

Also, in the sixties various scholars wrote directly on the Culture of Poverty model. For example, a short time after its formulation, Harrington described poor Americans as the "Other America." He noted that "the entire invisible land of the other Americans became a ghetto, a modern poor farm for the rejects of society and of the economy" (Harrington 1962:10). A more recent newspaper account by Leon Dash in the Washington Post, January 26-31, 1986, supports Harrington's view of the "Other America." Hence, he concluded that the location of his single teens study, Washington Highlands, is "A World Unto Itself" (Dash 1986:2). The year after Harrington described the Other America, Glazer and Moynihan also observed that low income blacks are part of the culture of poverty; for example, they found that black migrants to Harlem did not become part of the melting pot. Their non-assimilation resulted from "weak community ties, segregation, relatively low wages and comparable jobs, absence of a business class to create jobs, inadequate education, and clannishness based on state of origin" (Glazer and Moynihan 1963:26-27). Glazer and Moynihan also noted that "blacks were not a part of the melting pot because of family problems, including two few foster homes, poor housing and job conditions, broken homes, and children out of wedlock" (Glazer and Moynihan 1963:50-51). Beside, the Culture of Poverty model received attention in the study of multiple groups -- Anglo, Negro, and Spanish-speaking Americans (Irelan 1969:405-413).

Further, in the 1960s, scholars contributed to an important corollary of the Culture of Poverty model, the self-perpetuating nature of poverty. For example, Kenneth Clark noted that blacks are in a tangle of pathology. He wrote that "The dark ghetto is institutionalized pathology; it is chronic, self-perpetuating pathology; and it is the futile attempt by those with power to confine that pathology so as to prevent the spread of contagion to the "larger community" (Clark 1965:81). Clark noted that "not only is the pathology of the ghetto self-perpetuating, but one kind of pathology breeds another. The child born in the ghetto is more likely to come into a world of broken homes and illegitimacy; and this family and social instability are conducive to delinquency, drug addiction, and criminal violence" (Clark 1965:81). Two years later Moynihan again contributed to the Culture of Poverty model by focusing on the tangle of pathology suggested by Clark. While Clark was concerned with both the family and the ghetto as a community, Moynihan focused on the tangle of poverty in the family. Hence, he noted that the lower class Negro American is in a tangle of pathology closely related to family structure (Moynihan 1967:30). More specifically, he states that "Once or twice removed, it (the black family) will be found to be the principle source of most of the aberrant, inadequate or anti-social behavior that did not establish, but now serves to perpetuate the cycle of poverty and deprivation" (Moynihan 1967:30).

The Seventies

The Culture of Poverty model became useful to even more social science headings during the decade of the seventies. For example, social scientists writing on such topics as slum culture, urbanization, culture of poverty, and understanding poverty found Lewis useful in his poverty concept. Furthermore, the culture of poverty concept was used in the seventies for hypothesis testing (Rubenstein 1975:262; Kutner and Weeks 1977:340-41). Another interesting use of the Culture of Poverty model in the seventies is seen in the research in ethnic enclaves, including Chinatowns. For example, in their study of Chinatowns, Light and Wong concluded it appears that a "minority's adaptation to poverty will depend upon its mixture of vulnerable industries, invulnerable industries, welfare recipients, and the unemployed" (1975:1364).

Another reason the discussion of the Culture of Poverty model was expanded in the seventies is that it was in this decade that the model was extensively critiqued.

The Culture of Poverty Rebutted

Starting in the late sixties and continuing in the seventies, anthropologist Liebow (1967:223), sociologist Hylan Lewis (1967:338), anthropologists Stack and Valentine (1968:70) and sociologists Willie (1970:169), and Hill (1972:1) along with the scholars in Eleanor Leacock's The Culture of Poverty, critiqued the model and considered it inadequate.

To begin, according to Valentine, "much of the material found in the more recent literature on the "culture of poverty" and "lower-class culture" is prefigured in this, The Negro Family

11

in the United States, and other respected works by E. Franklin Frazier" (1968:19). It appears that one of Frazier's greatest contributions to the Culture of Poverty model is seen in his statement: "As a result of black migration (to turpentine and lumber camps and towns and cities) the Negro communities in the towns and cities in the South have long been characterized by widespread family disorganization" (1957:637). Frazier spoke of such pathologies as children born out of wedlock, lack of suitable living space and modern housing facilities, crime, delinquency, mental deficiency, and insanity (1 957:632-664). Regarding Frazier's interpretation of the status of urban blacks, Hill noted, "Despite the absence of data in Frazier's work indicating that disorganized patterns are characteristic of the majority of low-income blacks," social scientists, such as Glazer and Moynihan, continue to portray low income black family life as "typically" disorganized, patho-logical and disintegrating; others assert that a self-perpetuating "culture of poverty" exists among blacks. The great majority of black families, for example, are not characterized by criminal-ity, delinquency, drug addiction or desertion (1971:1). Willie, on the basis of family research in Syracuse, New York supports Hill's observations. Hence, "He had found there diversified behavior in rent payment practices and in family activities among households" which "cast doubt upon the concept of a culture of the poor" (1976:169-170). Willie also indicates there are deficiencies in all cultures "But these deficiencies should not be interpreted as an internally consistent normative and integrated pattern or as a system of beliefs that guide and give direction to behavior which perpetuates poverty" (1976:70-71).

There are also social scientists who disagree with the main corollary of the culture of poverty -- self-perpetuating poverty -- as noted by Oscar Lewis (1965:xliii) and Moynihan (1967:30). For example, Leibow countered that the cultural process that seems self-sustaining is "In part at least, a relatively small piece of social machinery which turns out, in rather mechanical fashion, independently produced look-alikes." Similarly, Hylan Lewis (1955:338) indicated that much of the behavior "Enmeshed in the culture of poverty is a response to facts of life." Carol Stack is even more explicit about her disagreement with the culture of poverty concept; she noted that "The structural adaptation of poverty described in her study of Jackson Harbor, a Midwestern town, does "Not lock people into a cycle of poverty preventing the poor from marrying, removing themselves from their kin network, or leaving town (1974:126). In this regard, Willie notes that "There is little information about the characteristics of affluent people who were once poor, and almost no comparative data betwen those kinds of families and those that continue in poverty over a number of years" (1970:322, 317).

Further, Valentine is critical of Lewis' methodology in Five Families, the Children of Sanchez, and La Vida, the basis for formulation of the Culture of Poverty model. One of his concerns is that Lewis, according to him, presents generalized descriptions of families in the introduction to his works, yet he "... does not intervene in the bulk of the volumes as either narrator or describer but simply presents a translated and edited form of his informants' words"; hence, to Valentine, "This makes the autobiographies seem almost like raw data, with all the problems of interpretation left to the reader" (1968:51). Valentine is also concerned with the representativeness of the families in Lewis' family studies. It resulted, he says, because Lewis indicates that "the Rio family is not presented here as a typical Puerto Rican family but rather as representative of one style of life in a Puerto Rican slum." According to Valentine, "The frequency distribution of this style of life cannot be determined until we have many comparable studies from other slums in Puerto Rico and elsewhere" (1968:52). Valentine also suggests "... that the subjects of La Vida were chosen, not because of their representativeness, but on the contrary, because they manifested deviant extremes (1968:53). Valentine says, "Note, for example, Lewis' statement that 'the Rio family is closer to the expression of an unbridled id than any other people I have studied" (1968:53). On the basis of Valentine's critique (1968), he states, "If it is true, as I have argued earlier, that the existence of a "culture of poverty" has not been convincingly demonstrated, then the concept does not constitute a valid support for either side of the ideological controversy" (Valentine 1968:70).

Support for the Culture of Poverty in the Seventies

Nevertheless, in the same decade research indicates support for the Culture of Poverty model. For example, using Leinwand's

Poverty and the Poor and Bernstein's, "The Distribution of Income in New York City," Ferrarotti noted that "Oscar Lewis' The Children of Sanchez and La Vida are referred to as helping toward a realistic understanding of the poor" (1972:1039). Ferrarotti also indicated that "Some statistics are given, e.g., that 15% of the residents of New York City live below the poverty line, and that increases in the percent of those earning $10,000 a year or over were almost exclusively concentrated among whites. Trends indicate that the rich are becoming richer and the poor, poorer" (1972:1039). Drawing on this research, Ferrarotti suggests that New York City's poor, as noted by Lewis, experiences a shortage of cash (1972:1039). Another example of support for Oscar Lewis' Culture of Poverty is Kerbo's work. Kerbo tested Lewis Coser's view "that the stigma of the welfare experience can lead to the problems of passive, dependent poor" among 103 welfare recipients receiving AFDC (1977:592). Kerbo found that recipients who blame the poor or victims for poverty experience feelings of stigma while recipients who accept a belief less critical of the poor, such as a religious explanation for poverty, "the recipient is found less likely to feel this stigma of public welfare support" (1977:592). Hence, Kerbo's work indicates that among the poor we find a sense of hope as well as a sense of helplessness. Perhaps the pro-culture of poverty and anti-culture of poverty scholars can find a common ground of scholarship by recognizing that both models are present in the culture of the poor. It is encouraging to find that hope exists among the poor, yet it appears to be pressing to eliminate fatalism and deprivation, an observation clearly verified by Carl Stokes, former Mayor of the City of Cleveland. Commenting on Edward C. Banfield's The Unheavenly City, Stokes noted that "Contrary to Banfield's findings, the urban crisis is real and the poor of our central cities are not better off now than ever before (1971:821). Although Stokes is in basic agreement with Banfield's view that urban poverty programs have failed, he does not agree with Banfield's position regarding "American ingenuity on the solvability of the problems" (1971:822). Stokes suggests that dilapidated, rat infested tenements, poor education, crime, family structure, and economics of the poor can be alleviated with less discrimination against black Americans, a large sum of money, and "a change of personal attitudes on the part of many Americans" (1971:822-825). Similarly Mogull noted that poverty persists because of "underemployment, in terms of number of weeks of full-time employment," (1972:164) and that Negroes and other nonwhites "are notoriously subject to high poverty probabilities" (1972:162). Mogull also noted that "Improved education, better health care and nutrition, pre-school preparation, school integration, equal rights for minorities and job training are all important routes to increasing labor force quality and employment" (1972:166). Hence, Stokes and Mogull not only recognize poverty as a condition of life for the poor, but they also recommend ways to make poverty self-correcting. Similarly, Edelstein indicates that she agrees with the importance of intervention "In the Poverty Cycle." The intervention strategy Edelstein notes is the establishment of a "comprehensive program that goes to the source - the young children and their families (1972:424). Furthermore, Edelstein notes that "The importance of intervening sufficiently early should give workers the impetus to push for long-lasting programs that help poor people move out of their apathy and become concerned about themselves and their children" (1972:424). Beside, Gans uses the Mertonian functional analysis, commonly associated with deviance, "to explain the persistence of poverty, and fifteen functions which poverty and the poor perform for the rest of American society, particularly the affluent, are identified and described" (1972:275).

What much of the research of the seventies indicates is that there is a culture of the poor however some poor maintain hope while other poor adopt an attitude of hopelessness. Hence, the findings of the seventies describe both sides of the ideological controversy around Oscar Lewis' culture of poverty. In general the findings present a balanced perspective; hence, there are social scientists who question the existence of a culture of poverty while other scholars not only verify its existence, but they also note the urgency of intervention strategies and the solvability of the problem.

Support for the Culture of Poverty in the Eighties

In the eighties the culture of poverty continues to receive considerable attention. For example, La Vida and The Children of Sanchez are often cited in this decade under such headings as Life in a Mexican Village, Families, Urbanization, Slum Culture, Understanding Poverty, and Patron-Client Relationships. In still other social science literature, varied scholars find the Culture of Poverty model useful, in varied ways, including policy making. For example, Oyemade notes that the Culture of Poverty model is one of four premises that guided the development of Head Start (1985:591). And, although "the basic assumptions of the antipoverty programs have been challenged, the problem of poverty remains a critical issue in American society today" (1985:599). For example, Oyemade noted that "The poverty rate in 1981 was 34.2% for blacks and 11.1% for whites, which represents an actual increase in poverty of black Americans rather than the projected decrease" (1985:599). Hence, the model has also influenced important policy between the subculture of the poor and the larger society. These existing studies of black unwed family life and the literature of both sides of the ideological controversy of the culture of poverty guided this study. Hence, the findings and the controversy encouraged us to conduct research that would probe the central issues in the literature of black family life as well as those not yet considered. To recapitulate, the findings indicate that the Culture of Poverty model has been important to the social sciences for almost three decades. In the sixties, emphasis was on the model, its main corollary, the self-perpetuating nature of poverty, and the poverty concept. In the seventies, social scientists often cited Lewis under various social science headings and used the model and data for hypothesis testing and studying ethnic enclaves in the US, such as Chinatowns, not commonly considered in the context of poverty. Another indication of the model's importance was the culture of poverty debate in the seventies; some anthropologists and sociologists questioned whether there is a culture of poverty while others noted its existence and indicated ways the poor can be extricated. Continuing in the eighties, the poverty concept is useful to varied social science subjects and it has been employed to suggest policy to help the poor. Insofar as the United States is concerned, Lewis perceived low-income blacks, Mexicans, Puerto Ricans, American Indians, and Southern poor whites as probably the largest sector of the culture of poverty (1965:li).

Setting

The poverty and single parent concerns have been tested in Tidewater, Virginia cities, Norfolk, Virginia Beach, Chesapeake, Portsmouth, Suffolk, and Hampton, Virginia. The larger setting for this study, has a high proportion of teen births to black females. For instance, in 1984, 95.1 percent of the state's teen out of wedlock births involved mothers between fifteen and nineteen years of age. Of this group, 55.9 percent were black (1984 Virginia Vital Statistics Annual Report.

Norfolk is the main research setting. Research among black single mothers was conducted in two of its housing developments, Young and Calvert Parks. Each residential area is comprised of public housing under the managing jurisdiction of the Norfolk Redevelopment and Housing Authority (NRHA). Minus the streets, Young Park is comprised of thirty-one acres, seventy-two brick cinder block buildings and 752 units of housing (150 one bedroom; 378 two bedroom; 224 three bedroom). Young Park was built under the United States Housing Act of 1949, Section 171. The buildings have concrete floors, vinyl tile and each of the 752 units cost $12,528 to construct. The units were first leased on August 26, 1953, and named for P. B. Young, a black man and publisher of the Norfolk Journal and Guide Newspaper. As of November 1986, there are 750 families in Young Park. Of this number 622 are single parents and their average, family, annual income is $5,565.00. On the other hand, Calvert Park is smaller. It is comprised of nineteen acres, minus the streets, thirty-two brick cinder block buildings, and 314 units of housing (58 one bedroom; 160 two bedroom; 96 three bedroom). Like Young Park, Calvert Park was built under the United States Housing Act of 1949, Section 171. The buildings have concrete floors and each unit was built at a cost of $12,950.00. The units were first leased effective May 23, 1957, and named for the street, which was the area of the development. Today, there are 312 families in Calvert Park; of this group, 262 are single parent families with an average annual income of $5,902.

Like the State of Virginia, in Norfolk, the urban research setting, the percentage of births to black teens is high. Because the vital statistics bureau in Virginia breaks the population down in cities by whites and nonwhites, it is only possible to give an impression of the extent of single motherhood among blacks in Norfolk (See Table 1). The nonwhite population includes not only a sizeable black population but also a rising Asian population. According to the 1980 U.S. Census, as determined by the Tayloe Murphy Institute, University of Virginia,

Charlottesville, in 1980, there were 266,979 people in Norfolk; 61 percent was white while 35 percent was non-white. As shown in Table 2, according to the Norfolk Pregnancy Hotline, using the Virginia Vital Statistics, in 1984, there were 964 births born to single teens in Norfolk. Twenty-three births were to teens under age fifteen to non-whites and none to whites. On the other hand of the 941 births to teens age 15 to 19, 528 (56.1 percent) were non-white while 413 (43.9 percent) were white. Another finding is that there were 535 abortions among Norfolk teens in 1984. In the age group under 15, 20 (3.7 percent) were non-white and 8 (1.5 percent) were white. Between age 15 and 19, 241 (45.0 percent) non-white and 266 (49.7 percent) white teens aborted. Also, there were 76 fetal deaths to girls age 15 to 19 in 1984; of this number 48 (63.2 percent) were nonwhite while 28 (36.8 percent) were white. And under fifteen there was only 1 fetal death -- experienced by a nonwhite teen. As these data indicate, the high percentage of births to nonwhite teens in Norfolk is closely related to the frequency of black, teen births on the state level.

Method

This book is Volume I of our single parents collection. It includes five studies about single, non-college fathers, single non-college mothers. Utilizing interview and participant observation data, Chapter Two describes single motherhood as forty-six women experienced it in 1971, in Norfolk, Virginia while Chapter Three, based on interviews, describes single motherhood from the perspective of forty-four single mothers in Tidewater, Virginia (Norfolk, Virginia Beach, Portsmouth, Hampton, Chesapeake, Hampton, and Suffolk) in 1978; also, it includes a 1981 questionnaire study of twenty-three expectant teens at the Norfolk, Virginia Coronado Vocational-Technical School for expectant mothers. On the other hand, Chapters Four and Five are based on interviews and autobiographies obtained during the spring and summer, in 1986, supplemented by observation information. Respondents for the 1986 studies were obtained by visiting courtyards and knocking on doors to apartments in Young Park and Calvert Park in Norfolk, Virginia. Chapters Six, Seven and Eight utilize the five studies to summarize the urban, black single parenthood experience, to compare black, single fatherhood with black, single motherhood, and suggest data-based pregnancy prevention models, respectively.

The specific methodology employed in each study is described in the related chapter. Starting with Chapter Two, interviews and participant observation are the data collection methods employed.

TABLE 1. Population, Norfolk, Virginia

1980/1985

Year	White and Non-White Population		
	Total	Percent White	Percent Non-White
1980	266,979	60.8	35.2
1985*	282,900	60-70	35-40

* The 1985 White and Non-White population estimated by the Norfolk Planning Commission

Source: Tayloe-Murphy Institute, University of Virginia, Charlottesville, Virginia

TABLE 2. Teenage Pregnancy, Norfolk, Virginia

1984

Categories	By Age				
	Under 15		15-19		Total
	Non-Whites	Whites	Non-Whites	Whites	
Births	23	0	528	413	964
Abortions	20	8	241	266	535
Fetal Deaths	1	0	48	28	77

Source: **Vital Statistics** Richmond, Virginia

Center for Health Statistics, 1984

20

CHAPTER TWO

UNWED SINGLE MOTHERS

Annie S. Barnes, Juanita Brown and Christine Forman

Introduction

Utilizing the findings of a 1971 study of single motherhood in two communities, Young Park, a subsidized, public, housing development and Cape Court (pseudonym), a working class neighborhood in Norfolk, Virginia, this chapter concerns interpersonal relations between single mothers and the fathers of their children and their quasi-boyfriends. Our focus is on sex, pregnancy, and survival strategies. We also test Malinowski's Principle of Legitimacy and Oscar Lewis' Culture of Poverty model to determine their relationship to urban, poor, black, single mothers in Norfolk, Virginia, in 1971. However, our primary concern is to use the findings to help develop the four data based pregnancy prevention models described in Chapter Eight.

Several questions guided the lines of inquiry. We asked, Why sex? Why pregnancy? What type of interpersonal relations existed between the respondents and the fathers of their children? What was the nature of relations between the respondents and their quasi-husbands/fathers? Does Malinowski's Principle of Legitimacy exist in Norfolk, Virginia? Do the findings support the culture of poverty?

Method

The data for this study were collected in 1971 by two of my students Juanita Brown and Christine Forman, in my Family course. Brown, at that time, was in her late twenties while Forman was in her early thirties. Though married, they were intensely interested in single parenthood and chose as the topic for their class research project, "Illegitimacy," the concept commonly used to describe children born out of wedlock as late as the early seventies. After I designed the interview

21

chedule, Brown designated the neighborhoods, Young Park, comprised of friends she had known since childhood, and Cape Court, then the location of her home. Brown knew all the respondents and Forman was soon acquainted with them. Because Brown had a long friendship with the women in Young Park and knew the women in Cape Court, both students found it easy to obtain interview and participant observation data for their single mothers' study that comprises this chapter.

Respondents' Background

Socioeconomic Characteristics

Forty-six black single mothers comprised our sample. Twenty-three lived in Cape Court, a working class neighborhood, while the remaining twenty-three lived in Young Park, a low income housing development. Thirty-one of the forty-six women were native to Norfolk, but fifteen migrated from two Virginia cities and the States of Alabama and North Carolina. Similarly, a majority of the fathers of their children were born in Norfolk; the migrant fathers were stationed at the Norfolk Navy Base and came from Michigan, North Carolina, Kansas, Texas, and Illinois. At the outset, we wish to note that sixteen of the respondents either were or had been married; hence, ten respondents lived with their husbands at the time of this study. Moreover, eleven had lived with their husbands as long as five years while two had lived with their husbands between six and ten years; moreover, two of the respondents had lived with their spouses eleven to fifteen years, and one eighteen years. Therefore, not only had slightly more than one third of the mothers experienced marriage, but for a relatively long time. While married, five did not have children, but eight had one or two children and three had three to six children. As a result, though approximately four fifths of the respondents became mothers between age fifteen and nineteen, eleven experienced giving birth to children fathered by their husbands.

We next desired to know why previously married respondents experienced separation or divorce. According to these respondents, complaints about their husbands' cruelty and extramarital relations, wife jealousy, physical abuse, different social interests, lack of love for husbands, and lack of financial support caused their marriages to break up. Though their former husbands, the women say, admitted their "undesirable actions" were the primary cause for marital failure, the men were critical of the women's constant nagging.

Because we desired an in-depth understanding of the women who comprise this study, our next task was to inquire about the characteristics of their parents. We found that approximately fifty percent of the respondents were children of parents whose principle source of income was welfare assistance, their education ranged from elementary through junior high school, and lived in Young Park. On the other hand, in Cape Court, a little over forty percent of the respondents were children of blue collar fathers, including longshoremen, merchant seamen, warehousemen, brakemen, and truck drivers. Their mothers worked as seamstresses, waitresses, and domestic laborers; and both parents earned an education that ranged between the eighth grade and a high school diploma. The other ten percent of the respondents were children of parents who were employed in postal work, management, the Navy, retail salesmanship, and floral designing. Their education ranged from tenth grade to a high school diploma and one father attended college one year. In summary, our respondents' parents represent a mixture of welfare and working class families.

Why Sex?

Before inquiring about single parenthood, we determined why the respondents engaged in sex. When the respondents were asked why, they gave varied reasons; the most frequent cause was "deep love for their boyfriends." Their love was evident in their constant desire to be with the men, continuous thoughts and conversations about them, happy feelings, and desire to satisfy their requests. The second most common cause was the desire for sex without regard for consequences. A number of the respondents explained that in their youth the desire for sex was frequent and potent; hence, the possible adverse effects of intercourse were superseded by intense desire. In still other cases, the respondents engaged in sex to conform to the standards of their friends or because their boyfriends "begged" or pressured them and they felt lonely and unloved. Moreover, they engaged in sex to retaliate against their strict parents; yet, one respondent reported that her first sex experience was with her father. She stated, "My father engaged in sex with me at an early age, consequently, I became confused and did not have high regard for morals." This finding suggests that mothers should be more observant of father-daughter relations. Because a few respondents needed clothing and a place to live, they engaged in sex with nonkinsmen.

Why Pregnancy?

After we learned why the respondents engaged in sex, we next asked them why they became pregnant. One important finding is that thirty of the women believed that, if they engaged in sex, they would possibly become pregnant. They had this feeling because they had been forewarned by their mothers, sisters, aunts, and foster mothers; however, only twelve had been told repeatedly not to engage in premarital sex. These respondents noted they were told not to engage in sex because it would lead to pregnancy, but they were not told of the consequences of pregnancy and single parenthood.

Thus, in general, the respondents had not participated in discussions regarding the benefits of high morals, disinterest of some males in females after sexual intercourse, their menstrual cycle, conception, contraception, and the vivid consequences of pregnancy without benefit of marriage, along with the burdensome task of taking care of children at an early age. One reason for inexposure to these discussions, the respondents say, was their parents' lack of courage and vocabulary "to bring up" such topics. Consequently, a few of the respondents became pregnant before they learned "where babies come from" or they did not now whether it was possible to get pregnant each time they had sexual intercourse. Another finding is that the respondents did not have sufficient knowledge and incentive to either use contraceptives or defer sexual gratification. In a few other cases, the women's boyfriends refused to use contraception because they wanted to "fully enjoy the sexual experience." However, one respondent's boyfriend told her that if she would engage in sex, he would protect her, but to her dismay, he failed to keep his promise.

Relationships

Interpersonal Relations with the Fathers of Their Children and Their Mothers

Reactions to pregnancy. The interpersonal relations the respondents experienced are vivid in their reactions to pregnancy. Also, to provide a complete description, the respondents described the reactions of their boyfriends to the onset of parenthood. When the respondents became pregnant, they experienced various reactions. For example, eighteen were happy because they thought it would cause their boyfriends to "really love" them. One of these respondents noted:

> I was afraid of my parents during my first pregnancy, but now that I am older, I feel that pregnancy is a nice experience for all young girls. I do not give a d... about people who knock it.

This comment suggests that unwed mothers may be a source of additional cases of single parenthood. A display of this attitudinal disposition could encourage teens to become mothers; hence, it would be wise for unmarried girls to select friends who are not single mothers.

Similarly, the males who impregnated the eighteen respondents were happy when they learned they were becoming fathers, but for different reasons than the respondents. The men were happy, the respondents reported, because they had proven themselves and thereby enhanced their masculinity. This finding suggests that single fathers are also a likely source of role models for male teens. That is, when they learn that some black men use making babies a criterion for manhood, they may use it to prove their own. However, the most serious point is that the respondents and their boyfriends had different motives for single parenthood; the respondents saw it as a means of enhancing their love relationship while their boyfriends saw it as a proving ground for manhood. It follows, as the respondents noted, that even the happy respondents were disappointed in motherhood.

From the beginning, the remainder of the sample was unhappy about pregnancy. Not only did some of the respondents react adversely to their first pregnancy, but there were mothers who also reacted adversely to their second and third pregnancies. For example, a respondent noted:

> The first time I was pregnant I did not tell the father of my child, because another girl was also carrying his child. The second time I became pregnant, initially, the father of my child denied it, but now he loves our child. During my third pregnancy, I wanted to marry the father of my baby, however, my mother prevented our marriage. As a result, I was confused and disturbed during all three pregnancies.

This case indicates that the mother experienced a number of difficulties, including deprivation of being the only one carrying a baby for her boyfriend, denial of fatherhood when she needed her boyfriend most, and parental interference.

Another reason the remaining twenty-eight women were unhappy about pregnancy and subsequent motherhood is that the fathers of their children were unkind toward fatherhood. According to the respondents, their boyfriends, upon learning they would become fathers, were dumbfounded, confused, unconvinced, and denied they were the fathers. What the respondents found was that impregnation decreased the men's interest in them; in fact, some boyfriends discontinued their relationships with the mothers of their children.

There were still other reasons that caused twenty-eight of the respondents to react adversely to motherhood. They included worry about dropping out of school because they suddenly realized their occupational and educational goals had to be abandoned. Also, they found it difficult to learn that a man does not necessarily love a woman more because she is carrying his baby. And they disliked being gossiped about and were sometimes jealous of their boyfriends because they shared few, if any, of their daily problems of shame, disgrace, and embarrassment. Even the single mothers who had experienced marriage as well as pregnancy out of wedlock tended to feel shame and guilt.

Furthermore, the twenty-eight respondents were unhappy about motherhood because they found children expensive, time consuming, confining and burdensome. Beside, it was often necessary to go to court to obtain child support. Even though eighteen of the forty-six mothers, initially considered single parenthood a happy experience, because of these problems, the entire sample noted that single motherhood is indeed a difficult and tragic experience.

Interpersonal Relations with Quasi-Fathers and Husbands

Though the women usually did not have the support of the fathers of their children, survival was related to their affiliation with other men. To help fill the gap in their lives, the women exchanged sexual privileges for emotional and economic support. For example, the men provided economic support, companionship, security, and a degree of happiness. They also performed fatherly duties; hence, they provided respondents with money to buy milk, food, clothing, pay rent, and engage in recreation; moreover, the men helped discipline their children and played with them. One respondent put it this way: "My boyfriend helps me with everything. He gives my children clothing and disciplines and plays with them. He is a father to my children in every sense of the word." Another respondent noted, "My third baby's father is my boyfriend. He is just like a father to all three of my children." These findings indicate that, when the Norfolk women became mothers, they needed men who were their husbands and the fathers of their children. Because of their inaccessibility, the economic and emotional gap as well as the responsibilities of rearing children and maintaining a home required the presence of a quasi father-husband.

In Retrospect

We asked the respondents what they would do if they could start life over with their present knowledge. In response, except for one mother, they noted they would stay in high school and college and refrain from sex because they had learned that one can live without it. According to them, the desire for sex would be "fought" by diverting their energy into worthwhile activities, including education and recreation. In the event their sexual desires overpowered them, they would use contraceptives and sleep with only responsible men; men who would make good husband-father providers. Furthermore, some of the respondents noted that, if their boyfriends asked them to engage in sex, providing the men were financially stable, they would suggest marriage.

Though the respondents indicated they would take these precautionary measures, they felt very strongly that the major responsibility for preventing daughters from bearing children rests with mothers. For example, the respondents noted that single parenthood could either be prevented or decreased if mothers engage their daughters constantly, at an early age, in two way conversation about sex. Such discussions, they say, should permit daughters, without condemnation, to ask varied questions. The respondents also think that mothers should be less strict and refrain from accusing them of sex without adequate proof. If mothers find their daughters are sexually active, in their opinion, they should refrain from calling them bad names; instead, they should determine how their daughters can effectively deal with their desire for sex. Moreover, the respondents indicated that mothers should instruct their daughters to abstain from premarital sex and inform them of contraception. For example, one respondent suggested that mothers tell their daughters:

> Do not participate in sex. Abstinence is the best policy. If you feel that you cannot exist without sex, get married. If you can neither get married nor abstain from sex, use contraceptives, such as vaginal gels, the pill, the loop, or have your tubes tied.

Hence, parental and child responsibility, according to the respondents, can decrease the frequency of black single parenthood.

Discussion

This analysis of single parenthood in two residential areas in Norfolk, Virginia, in 1971, is used to discuss interpersonal relations between mothers and the men important to their family life. To begin, in general, we found that a majority of respondents and fathers of their children were native to Norfolk; others were in the U.S. Navy. When the women became mothers of their children, they were in their teens or they had married and separated or divorced. Hence, these findings indicate that, beside teens, another problem is that separated and divorced women sometimes bear children by men who are not their husbands. A possible result is that single mothers may serve as role models for young girls who either replicate their pattern or merely risk pregnancy because older women bear children out of wedlock.

Another pattern is that, prior to separation or divorce, the eleven once married respondents had experienced varied problems with their husbands in marriage. Hence, they experienced husband cruelty, husband extramarital relations, wife jealousy, wife abuse, different social interests, weak emotional bonds, and inadequate financial support. These findings indicate that the respondents experienced wife abuse in interpersonal relations with their husbands and single motherhood at various stages of their lives.

After looking at their family background, we found that about half of the respondents represented families receiving public assistance while the remainder came from working class families. Perhaps this signals the importance of understanding all facets of single parenthood and implementing intervention strategies that eliminate single parenthood across black social classes.

When we note why the respondents engaged in sex and became pregnant, we can start by devising effective strategies. The respondents engaged in sex because of deep love for their boyfriends, a strong desire for sex, without regard for consequences, low self esteem, rebellion against parents who were trying to protect them from a difficult life, boyfriend and father pressure (one case), and economic needs. Some other respondents became pregnant because their boyfriends refused contraception and the respondents lacked knowledge and incentive to use contraception and restraint. In still other cases, the respondents became pregnant because they allowed their desires to overrule the warnings from their families and their parents did not implement proper childrearing techniques.

Once the respondents became pregnant, the lives of a majority changed immediately. Except one mother, soon thereafter all respondents changed their minds about motherhood. Hence, in the beginning, some respondents were happy about the onset of motherhood, because they believed it would enhance relations with their boyfriends, a view that could serve as a model for young girls. On the other hand, a majority became unhappy immediately because their boyfriends denied fatherhood, parents interfered (one), and men became less interested or discontinued their relationships. Also, it was not only necessary to abandon their educational goals, but it was often difficult to obtain child support, and child care was expensive, time consuming, confining, and a hindrance. Except one female, the respondents noted that it was a tragic experience. They survived it, they say, with the assistance of men who served as quasi fathers-husbands; they helped fill the economic and emotional gap in their lives and assisted with child support, care, and rearing.

These findings caused us to ask the respondents, in retrospect, what they would do if they could live their lives over with their present knowledge. According to forty-six respondents, they would not become single mothers. Instead, they would complete their high school training and obtain a college education, restrain their sexual desires, use contraception, and only participate in sex with men who would make good husbands.

Though they would take these precautions, according to the respondents, the burden of responsibility for preventing pregnancy, in the first place, is with mothers. Hence, they suggest frequent discussions, void of condemnation and name calling, between mothers and their daughters, and solutions to their sex problems. Also, the findings suggest moderate parental strictness and instruction in use of contraception and consequences of pregnancy and single parenthood.

Principle of Legitimacy

This study is also instructive about the existence of Malinowski's Principle of Legitimacy in Norfolk, Virginia. Although at first it may appear that this sociological law does not exist in Cape Court and Young Park, it is highly evident. There are several examples that support this observation. One example concerns the respondent who was afraid of her parents. If single parenthood had been acceptable, fear would not have existed. Two other examples that illustrate the existence of the legitimacy norm in Young Park and Cape Court are the adverse reactions of mothers to their daughter's pregnancy and neighbor's gossip. Still another indication is that the respondents felt guilt and shame. Moreover, because some fathers were unkind toward fatherhood -- even to the extent of denying paternity -- it is also clear that some single fathers did not condone their own single parenthood. We thus concluded that single parent is not synonymous with absence of the Principle of Legitimacy; in effect, the single mothers recognized the existence of the law by their own reactions to single motherhood.

Culture of Poverty

As noted in Chapter One, Oscar Lewis has described the culture of poverty on the subculture and family level. Our first task is to determine whether single mothers in Young Park and Cape Court, in 1971, conformed to the Culture of Poverty model on the subculture level. Lewis has noted varied poverty traits, including deprivation on the subculture level (1965). The Norfolk mothers support this characteristic; for example, they were deprived of adequate husband-father economic support. However, they obtained it from men who assumed the roles of quasi- husbands and fathers (Schulz 1970:234) in exchange for sexual favors. Also, there are two principal ways the respondents correspond to the culture of poverty on the family level, including absence of a long and protected childhood. Hence, four-fifths of the respondents became mothers between fifteen and nineteen years of age. Also, male-abandonment of their children and the women who birthed them is another trait in their sample that corresponds to the culture of poverty. Therefore, we concluded that our study supports the Culture of Poverty model on both the subculture and family level.

However, as mentioned earlier, our primary concern is with the picture of poverty on the subculture, communal, family and individual level for the purpose of developing a self-correcting poverty model, a self-correcting single parenthood model, and a pregnancy - prevention model. Hence, in Chapter Seven and Chapter Eight, using Oscar Lewis' work as a research guide, we utilized the findings in this study to help alleviate poverty and single parenthood.

An earlier version of this chapter was presented at the 1973 meeting of the Southern Anthropological Society, Virginia Polytechnic Institute and State University; and a taped interview was distributed by Virginia Polytechnic Institute and State University to twenty-six radio stations.

CHAPTER THREE

WHY SINGLE MOTHERHOOD?

Introduction

As shown in Chapter one, for several decades the literature has called attention to black, single motherhood. And, as noted in Chapter Two, my students and I began conducting research among black single mothers in 1971. Seven years later, in 1978, we conducted another study and, in 1981, we studied teens expecting their first child. The last two studies comprise this chapter. Our aim is to describe the causes, reactions, and solutions to single parenthood, test Malinowski's Principle of Legitimacy, relate Oscar Lewis' Culture of Poverty model to Tidewater, Virginia, single mothers, and suggest addenda to the model and a Self-Correcting Poverty proposition. Further, as shown in Chapter Eight, the findings are used to develop pregnancy prevention models.

Methodology

The major sources of data cited throughout this chapter are an interview study conducted among forty-five single mothers, as part of a larger study about black women, in the fall of 1978, and a questionnaire study implemented during the spring of 1981 among twenty-three high school teens expecting their first child. These data are supplemented with interview information from a teacher-respondent, not included in the single, mother's sample, in the Coronado Vocational-Technical School in Norfolk. During a decade and a half, this teacher has taught or encountered several hundred expectant teens. Our interview took place in her classroom; upon its completion, the respondents arrived for class, which gave me an opportunity to see some of them. Following our interview, the teacher conducted the questionnaire study among the twenty-three young women. When using data from these questionnaires, I shall identify it as the teen sample while the data from the adult sample, excluding the teacher respondent, will be identified as sample or adult sample. The teen study was conducted especially to clarify certain findings in the adult sample and was not intended as an independent study. Hence, the adult sample is larger and comprises the major part of this chapter. As a footnote to the methodology, even though all the respondents in the adult sample are single mothers, the questions were phrased to ask them what they considered causes, reactions, and solutions without asking them to answer the questions on the basis of their own experience. However, a basic assumption is that they responded according to their own lives; on the other hand, the teen sample was asked to describe their personal experience as expectant mothers.

Backgrounds of Samples

The teen sample is comprised of twenty-three young women who were expecting their first child and ranged in age from fourteen to eighteen years. Correspondingly, their educational level ranged from the sixth to the twelfth grade. The data indicate that, when the teens reached the ninth grade, oncoming motherhood maintained a steady increase through the eleventh grade, but in their senior year, the frequency of becoming an expectant mother decreased to the tenth grade level.

The adult sample is comprised of forty-four unwed mothers in the Tidewater cities (Norfolk, Virginia Beach, Chesapeake, Portsmouth, Suffolk, and Hampton) obtained in the fall of 1978. The respondents ranged in age from twenty to over forty years of age, and thirteen obtained less than a high school education; yet, thirty-one single mothers achieved a high school diploma or a higher level of education. Of the thirty five others who provided their job affiliation, fourteen were clerical and service workers and twelve were unemployed while six were managers or officials. In general, the single mothers were either unemployed or worked in low paying jobs, yet six had realized employment success.

Regarding their income, only six respondents were welfare recipients while twenty-six received between $3,999 and $6,999 and four women earned between $7,000 and $12,999 annually. Though our economic data are incomplete because some respondents consider it private, these findings indicate that, contrary popular belief, there are single mothers without welfare assistance; yet, they confirm the existence of poverty. For example, twenty mothers had three to seven or more children; hence, almost half of the sample and their children lived close to the nonfarm poverty level, $6,600 for a family of four in 1978.

Why Single Motherhood?

We found that black females, in Tidewater, are influenced by various individuals to become single mothers. After classifying and organizing the data, we found that the respondents noted several categories of individuals who contribute to single parenthood. They include mothers, grandmothers, males, peers, and young females, themselves. Starting with mothers, the respondents noted that maternal failure to repeatedly discourage their daughters from bearing children outside marriage results in single parenthood.

Another mother oriented reason, the sample reported, for single motherhood, is that black women do not adequately teach their daughters about menstruation and consequences of sex. One respondent, a supervisor in the American Cross Office in Tidewater, cited the extent that youth lack such knowledge. She noted that, in a human sexuality class, she taught in her church, many of the teenagers thought pregnancy could only occur if both partners reached a climax; further, the girls were not aware they could get pregnant at any time of the month; nor did they know the scientific terms for male and female genitals. Because sometimes they are not sufficiently informed, a discussion of sex has long been a closed issue in some black families. In many cases, the only teachers our children have is peer groups. Another reason that black children are underinformed about sex is because we often believe that being informed is a license for sexual behavior.

Similarly, some of us do not want schools to teach our children about sex, menstruation, contraception, impregnation, and its consequences. Yet, many pregnancies are related in some way to school activities, an observation amply verified by our teacher-respondent at the Coronado Vocational-Technical School for pregnant girls. For example, she explained that after recounting girls' pregnancies related either directly or indirectly to school. The girls usually get pregnant, she said, at vacation time, especially Christmas and Easter, as well as in the summer, and during basketball, football, and prom seasons. This finding seems to encourage parents and school systems to take an active role in child rearing by establishing birth control clinics in junior and senior high schools and teaching black females sex power. If the instruction is effective, the girls are likely to use it during all seasons, including vacation time.

Another mother related cause of single motherhood is hostility between mothers and their daughters. Because daughters know their parents are embarrassed, they bear children to get even with them. It is likely their hostility toward their mothers developed, because they attempted to keep them from participating in particular activities. When the girls could not get their way, on purpose, they became pregnant. Because almost half (twenty) of the forty-four respondents noted that single parenthood often resulted from the desire of young girls to get even with their mothers, training for parenthood is necessary to curtail single motherhood. Parents can be taught how to discipline and the danger signals that indicate the need to curtail disciplining. With such knowledge, even though girls may engage in sex, they will be less likely to bear children. Nonetheless, it is disadvantageous for girls to curtail their own joy of youth and settle into adulthood prematurely to get even with their mothers. There are positive ways they can express hostility, including excellent leadership, participation in varied wholesome organizations, and utilization of black female sex and blood power; that is, sexual abstinence, male pleading without yielding, infrequent sex, total commitment to contraception with sex, and sex-delay after the promise -- change of mind, if there is reservation, anti-sex aggressiveness, and uninterrupted, perpetuation of the monthly menstrual cycle. Sex power in one young black woman is more powerful than all the hostility that 100 girls can direct toward their mothers. We call this self-sex and menstruation control; black female sex power. Moreover, young females can use their energies to help develop themselves into highly achieving, prideful, and refined young women -- goals that will stand them in good stead for life. The underlying argument here is that young black women should love themselves too much to interrupt their happiness; instead, they should become young women with power -- youth who subordinate sex to morality, effective family relations, and all types of school achievements.

According to the sample, mother permissiveness is another cause of single motherhood. Hence, the respondents noted that a few mothers encourage their daughters to engage in sexual activity. One Tidewater mother, for example, permitted her thirteen year old daughter to date a fifty-five year old man. She would not allow him to move into their apartment, but she permitted the girl to visit his apartment. In return, the man paid the mother and daughter's rent and bought all their clothes and food. Moreover, during the school term, he took her to school in the mornings and returned her home in the afternoons. Not only did he make her the best dressed girl in school, but he fully supported his child that she had mothered.

Another reason the respondents gave for single motherhood is grandmothers' orientation toward grandchildren born to their daughters. For example, their participation in the child-rearing process, the respondents say, contributes to women becoming mothers more than one time. The teen sample indicates now extensively grandparents are expected to help with childrearing. Thus, thirteen expected their mother and twelve expected their baby's paternal grandmother to help with child care while nine teens expected the prospective fathers to also help with child care. With multiple assistance, the young mothers have not experienced as much drudgery, as they would have, if grandparental help had not been available. Another finding is that black grandparents encourage motherhood twice or more additional times by allowing their daughters and grandchildren to live with them. In all probability, if young women, no matter how young, were required to get their own residence, upon the birth of their first child, they would be careful not to bear another. Why? Because the difficulty of motherhood would be realized to its fullest. Since it is traditional in our families to take in relatives, indeed, it is hard for black parents to tell their unmarried daughters with children they must find new living quarters. There is a certain feeling of guilt we experience when we do not share our homes with relatives. The respondents had also found that the practice of grandparents displaying a great deal of happiness over their grandchildren, born out of wedlock, encourages single parenthood. Another way grandparents contribute to out of wedlock births, the respondents say, is by adopting their grandchildren while a few respondents noted that when grandparents make financial contributions to their daughter and grandchild, they encourage their daughters to again experience motherhood.

A third cause of single motherhood is male oriented. For example, according to the respondents, varied groups of church men contribute to single motherhood. They noted that "because of hypocrisy in the church, more and more Holiness, Baptist, and Methodist teen church members are getting pregnant." They say for example, "that ministers and deacons contribute to unwed sex and pregnancy." According to two respondents, they know ministers who propositioned church teens and another reported, "I know a deacon who fathered a child by one of our teen, church members. They 'turned' her out of the church, but they let him remain on the deacon board." When male religious leaders proposition and impregnate teens they are setting an example for younger male teens, hence, it is incumbent upon religious leaders to refrain from sexual behavior with church members, especially teenage girls.

On a larger scale, younger men also contribute to single parenthood. For example, they give young girls misinformation about their fecundity. In Tidewater, they tell girls, "I won't make you pregnant because I got hurt and cannot make babies," and "I had the mumps late which caused me to be unable to make babies." Or, they give them misinformation about contraception techniques, and times one can get pregnant. For example, the Tidewater young men tell girls, "You can't get pregnant the first time you have sex," and "You can't get pregnant every day in the month; this is the time of the month that women don't get pregnant." Also, they tell girls that aspirins and feminine hygiene are effective, post, intercourse, contraceptive measures. Further, they tell them saran wrap substitutes for condoms and that the withdrawal technique is as effective as contraception.

For example, five of the expectant teens became pregnant because of contraception misinformation. Though contraception misinformation contributed to single motherhood, the adult sample did not consider it a major factor. On the other hand, they agreed that pregnancy occurred because of accidents with contraception.

37

The adult sample also noted another male oriented cause, pressure from an assortment of men, that leads to single parenthood. According to the respondents, ten to fifteen year old girls are pressured into having sex by the man across the street or the man next door. The initial step is that a man sees a girl who needs money or clothes and makes them available with no apparent obligation. Sometime later, he approaches the girl for sexual favors, when she refuses him, he reminds her that he has been good to her and that she should "give him what he wants." According to the respondents, this approach causes girls to reciprocate.

Another male oriented cause for single parenthood occurs in the home. Often boyfriends of mothers or stepfathers of girls request sexual favors. When left alone in the home, the men pressure their stepdaughters and their girlfriends' daughters to engage in sex and, in fewer cases, the respondents say, fathers engage in sex with their daughters. In all cases, the respondents say, the girls are afraid to tell their mothers because the women become angry and "put them out of the house." Nevertheless, some of the girls tell their mothers and are forced to leave home; hence, mothers place more confidence in what their boyfriends and husbands say than in what their daughters report. This finding suggests that not only should mothers pay more attention to what their daughters say, but also to relationships between their daughters and their own male friends. An example is Maria (See Chapter One), a Norfolk single mother who lives with a military officer. She explained to him that he should not approach her teenage daughter. In the event it occurs, she will believe her daughter and discontinue their courtship. Indeed, this woman is a model for other women with live in boyfriends and husbands who are stepfathers to their children.

Also, in the home, there is another male oriented cause of single parenthood. It relates to blood relatives, especially uncles and cousins. This occurs when families take in male relatives. According to a respondent, usually, when the families give parties, "the male relatives encourage their nieces and cousins to drink alcoholic beverages and take advantage of them." Even though girls do not usually get pregnant, the respondents say, their relatives help make them sexually active, which sometimes leads to single parenthood.

Another male oriented cause of single parenthood is rape by acquaintances. For example, according to a respondent, because a fifteen year old girl's birth control pills made her sick, the doctor advised her to use a different kind. On her way to the doctor's office, to get the prescription, she visited a girl-friend who was on the pill. While there, a male neighbor and father of two children, by his wife, asked them to sit on his porch and talk. In the absence of his family, they visited him and, unknowingly drank a drugged soda, which caused them to pass out. Then, according to the respondent, he put both girls in bed, raped them alternatively and waited for them to wake up. Though the girl who was on the pill did not get pregnant, her friend became pregnant. Because the girl's mother thought that her boyfriend had made her pregnant, she constantly abused the girl. Since the girl knew her brother would either kill or hurt the father of her child, she delayed telling her mother the name of the child's father until her brother joined the army. Once the mother learned who the father was, she helped her daughter and when the baby was born, it was put up for adoption. This case at least implies that single mother-hood is not the norm among all black low income families; similarly, four expectant teens did not want to get pregnant. Both findings support the principle of legitimacy.

Still another male related cause of single parenthood is the black, male macho. In some Tidewater, young, black, male groups, a criterion of maleness is frequent sex. After a while, this criterion is replaced with another norm, proof of sexual activity, a baby. The first young man who impregnates a girl becomes its leader, and he teases his friends until they measure up to his standards. Subsequent group leadership shifts to the member who fathers the largest number of children. Some-times he had as many as seven or eight children and has been known to get two girls pregnant about the same time. If the mothers of their children attend the same school, especially the Coronado Vocational School, while talking about the father of their child, they learn from each other they are soon to become mothers of the same man's children.

Next, young girls also become pregnant to conform to peer norms. Our girls must become convinced of morally acceptable behavior and only implement their convictions. When they lose their friends because they abstain from sex, they should realize they are winners and sexually powerful.

Beside mothers, grandparents, men, and peers, young women contribute to their own single motherhood. For example, one trait, the respondents say, is insufficient control over their sex desires -- lack of sex power. That is, they have not learned that, instead of letting their sex desires control them, they must take charge of their bodies. When they learn and implement this lesson, if they engage in sex, they are more likely to use contraception; and they will enjoy power over their sexuality. For example, Maria, a welfare mother explained that she is poor and the only thing she truly has power over is her sex. Therefore, since bearing her child, less than two decades ago, she has never missed a menstrual cycle; she calls this sex power. Moreover, though she lives with a military officer, he must plead, provide expensive gifts, demonstrate kindness, and provide ample economic support before she obliges his sex requests. Even then, she says, only rearely are his requests honored; however, after she makes him a promise, she is the proud recipient of much pleasure as she observes his apparent happy anticipation. The respondent literally cherishes sex and menstrual power -- perpetual, monthly, menstrual cycles; indeed, she exercises sex and blood power and only engages in sex with one man three or four times a month. Though poor, she says, she is not powerless. Surely, power over one's sexuality is far more powerful than single motherhood. When black women develop sex and blood power, they will demonstrate control over themselves, unswerving contraception dedication, sexual abstinence, proper circumstances, rewards, and absence of pregnancies. With widespread sex and blood power, black women will obtain social honor in society as well as among their own people, especially among their men, and achieve success and prosperity as well as enhanced bonding with other black women, black men, and the entire society.

According to the respondents, another female related cause for single parenthood is low self esteem. By low self esteem the respondents mean that one does not think enough of herself to keep her reputation, love relationship, and schooling in tact. Black young women also demonstrate low self esteem when they desire a souvenir (baby) from lovers who have deserted them. It occurs, unbeknowing to lovers, when their ex-girlfriends provide them sexual pleasures. Interestingly, even after men discontinue their relationship with some Tidewater women, sex continues.

Similarly, the respondents say, another female related reason for bearing children out of wedlock is self esteem enhancement. That is, the adult respondents noted that, becoming a single mother, gives an otherwise depraved women, a possession. This point is supported by the teen sample; hence, five became pregnant because they desired someone to love and three wanted to be needed. These young women suggest that the male-female relationship is not sufficiently rewarding and that only a by-product, a child, brings fulfillment. One solution is to teach youth how to experience quality boy-girl relationships. Another solution is to help them become convinced of the need to enhance their self esteem on the basis of societal norms -- achievement in education and work -- instead of using personal and peer standards, especially child-bearing.

Then, another female related reason why our girls become single mothers it that they engage in sex because they fear loosing their boyfriends. For example, the Coronado teacher-respondent related that girls' boyfriends insist they "Go all the way or risk loosing them." What young women need to be taught is that, if they lose young men, because they abstain from sex, in time, they will lose them anyway. Moreover, young women should retort, if you do not stop pressuring me to engage in sex, you risk loosing me; beside, if you loved me, you would not ask me to engage in sex and risk my happy, young, single life. Also, if you loved me, you would not ask me to engage in sex and disappoint Mama and Daddy, my best friends. When girls become convinced of the accuracy of these statements and use them, unswervingly, they will possess sex power; and learn that premarital sex is everything, but sex power.

Beside, another female oriented reason for single motherhood is that young women want to get pregnant. This finding is supported by the teen sample; nine of the girls became pregnant by choice. This attitude may account, in part, for some young men's failure to support their children and the mothers of their children. Hence, in the final analysis, unwed fathers are labeled as irresponsible; correspondingly, when young women become impregnated, unbeknowing to their boyfriends, or ask them to help make babies, we need to focus on black women's irresponsibility and self esteem.

In addition, the desire for income, on the part of young women and young men, leads to single parenthood. Among the forty-four unwed mothers, twenty-two or half of them agreed that it accounts for some cases of single parenthood. What we suggest, is that cutting off welfare payments is important, but equally important is the need to instill in young black men and young black women the conviction to work for their own money and refrain from making babies as a source of income. On the other hand, because half of the respondents disagreed, it is apparent that childbearing does not always relate to public assistance.

Hence, there are also girls, especially between age fifteen and seventeen, according to the teacher-respondent, who become single mothers to obtain support from the fathers of their children and not from the government, a point not mentioned in commentaries about single mothers. A case in point is a seventeen year old girl who drove a Mark V car to high school and said, "Whatever I want, I get because I am pregnant" while another seventeen year old girl stated, "I'm pregnant because I am smart. My boyfriend, a longshoreman, puts money in a savings account for me and also gives me a U.S. Savings Bond each pay day and soon he will give me a new debt-free Volkswagen." This finding suggests that black women are willing to become single mothers to obtain private sources of income. As we recall, the male neighbors also used money as bait to obtain sexual favors. These findings seem to suggest the importance of training young women not to take money and goods from the government and men and not to give in to pressure for sexual favors. Again, they should be told that the keys to success are sex and blood power, a good education, and hard work in outstanding jobs.

Reactions to Becoming Single Mothers

Upon finding the causes of single motherhood, our concern focused on the reactions of our women to becoming single mothers. Because we frequently hear that blacks are proud to become single parents, I abstracted the forty-four single mothers from our larger women's study to determine their views of single parenthood. What I found is that, though fourteen disagreed and five did not express an opinion, over half of the respondents noted that it is a happy experience. Yet more than a third indicated that it causes deprivation and shame -- experienced when neighbors gossip. Of the forty-four mothers, twenty-five stated that both shame and inconvenience are also associated with single motherhood while ten disagreed and nine did not give an opinion. This finding is corroborated by other data in our study; hence, one respondent noted that even though single parenthood appears to be the norm in certain communities, it is not an approved pattern. When I asked for justification, she related that, as soon as girls become pregnant, neighbors begin gossiping. Certainly, if neighbors gossip, there is an underlying norm that does not condone single parenthood even when it seems acceptable. Our teacher-respondent explained that "Shame was greater because of betrayal of family trust than outside opinions. The family often ostracizes the girl, she says, which lets her know they have been hurt by her actions." She continued, "It is most evident in sibling behavior; initially, the girl's brothers refuse to speak to her and sometimes later her sisters begin to treat her the same way." As seen in the teen sample, shunning was verified by three respondents; they were shunned by their friends and sisters.

Another finding is that unwed motherhood causes emotional strain. According to the respondents, young Tidewater unmarried mothers are immature, as seen in their playful behavior and failure to take all the responsibilities of motherhood. A related finding is that they experience emotional strain. For example, in the teen sample, seventeen of the girls worried about their unborn child's well being while five experienced verbal abuse because their mothers constantly complained about the shame they had caused their family, and experienced depression. Moreover, there is social strain, the adult respondents say, because young unmarried mothers want to have fun like other girls their age, but there are times when they must remain home to care for their children. Financial strain is still another problem, for often girls drop out of junior and senior high school, though unprepared, to earn a living. They find it difficult to obtain medical attention, clothes, food, and bedding for their children and inevitably end up on welfare rosters.

However, as noted earlier, over half the adult sample considered single parenthood a happy experience. Consequently, our next task was to analyze additional data from the teen sample and their teacher. It was found that the most frequent reaction, among the teens, was also happiness; moreover, the girls in this category were usually between the age fifteen and seventeen. It should be made clear, however, that some girls in this age group, their teacher says, were very unhappy, shame, sad, confused, and disappointed. It is, thus, noteworthy that nine girls were sad, hurt, confused or undecided about their state of mind.

The findings of the two samples verify each other. On one hand, half of the respondents in each sample considered single motherhood a happy experience. On the other hand, except two teens, the teen sample noted problems and the adult sample provided evidence to support the view that single motherhood is an unhappy experience. For example, they noted that secrecy about pregnancy, as long as possible, and emotional and financial strain were experienced by girls, boy hatred, and family ostracization were problems of single mothers. Further, according to the adult respondents, unwed mothers, their children, and their parents are stigmatized. It, indeed, seems clear that unwed pregnancy and motherhood have different effects on different females. Furthermore, in view of the findings, it is likely that children will bear the major burden of improper birth. The most vivid memories probably begin somewhere around age three or four years when playmates threaten to tell their fathers about their disagreements. It is perhaps, then, they begin to realize they have started life a step behind the rest of the world, because when arguments arise at play, they can only retort they will tell their mothers, less respected disciplinarians than fathers. And when children born out of wedlock live in neighborhoods where numerous children have the same birth status, the realization they are a step behind their other peers may come somewhat late in life. Moreover, children will bear the burden of improper birth in social conversation, family history, contact with relatives and friends, and in the workplace, especially in the job application process; in fact, for most children born out of wedlock, the burden of improper birth is a lifelong problem.

Single motherhood is not only traumatic for some young Tidewater mothers, but it is also traumatic for grandparents. It was found that it causes them, including the mothers of unwed fathers, shame. For example, according to a respondent, a low income mother in Young Park who had constantly gossiped about unwed mothers in this neighborhood kept her son's two out of wedlock children a secret, as long as possible, a usual reaction when single parenthood is not an acceptable event of life. Once the neighbors found out, they began talking and she constantly shared her shame with one of them.

On the basis of our findings, we concluded that single motherhood results in varied reactions and becomes a complex situation. Yet, it appears that, when understood, as noted by our respondents, solutions are available and workable, if the society -- community, churches, and civic groups -- work with our youth (See Chapter Eight).

Discussion

One concern of this chapter was causes of single parenthood in Tidewater, Virginia, including Norfolk. We noted five categories of individuals who contribute to single parenthood; mothers, grandmothers, males, peers, and young females, themselves. Starting with mothers, the respondents noted they contribute to their daughters single parenthood because they do not adequately discourage it, provide sex education, and encourage sex education in the schools. Also, mother-daughter hostility and mother permissiveness contribute to single parenthood. Next, the respondents noted that grandmothers enhance single parenthood several ways. For example, it is achieved by participating in the childrearing process and expressing happiness. Also, according to the respondents, men, including church leaders, contribute to black single parenthood. They relate that not only do they engage in sex with young church girls, but one respondent knew a deacon who impregnated a young girl in their church. However, younger males seem to contribute more extensively to single parenthood than parents, grandparents, and church leaders. Hence, boyfriends give girls misinformation about their fecundity and contraception while male neighbors, especially the man across the street or next door, provide gifts of money and clothing for their young neighbors and later request sexual favors. Beside, boyfriends of mothers, girls' stepfathers, and a few fathers request young girls to engage in sex while at home alone, but mothers usually fail to listen to their daughters or require them to find some place else to live. According to the respondents, uncles also contribute to sexual development, if not pregnancy of their young nieces; moreover, the respondents say, the black, male macho is another element in sex and pregnancy. These findings seem to indicate that training in human sexuality is the answer to a majority of the problems leading to single motherhood in Tidewater. Hence, the second aim in this study is to recommend solutions to single parenthood (See models in Chapter Eight).

Principle of Legitimacy

Furthermore, the findings in this study support Malinowski's Principle of Legitimacy. Goode notes that "Malinowski was stating a proposition about a cultural element: he asserted that the norm would always be found, not that the members of the society would obey it under specified conditions" (1960). Though there is single parenthood in Tidewater, the legitimacy principle is evident in gossip among neighbors and shame experienced by a single father's mother, as well as shame, guilt, unhappiness, sadness, confusion, disappointment, secrecy about pregnancy as long as possible, and family shunning experienced by single mothers.

Support for the Culture of Poverty

We also found that the Tidewater, Virginia, black, single, parent respondents in this chapter support Oscar Lewis' culture of poverty on the subculture and individual level. Lewis noted that on the subculture level its characteristics include violence and death, suffering, deprivation, infidelity, broken homes, delinquency, corruption, police brutality, and cruelty among the poor (1965:xii). Among the Tidewater respondents, as reported by almost half of both samples, suffering was noted in shame, inconvenience of parenthood, emotional strain, suffering. Similarly, deprivation is another characteristic experienced by the respondents; they were deprived of academic and occupational achievement and attempted to obtain the love of their boyfriends and children as possessions and substitutions for educational and occupational achievement. Moreover, on the individual level of the culture of poverty, as noted in Chapter One, another characteristic of the poor is low self esteem (Schulz 1970); the willingness of Tidewater respondents to bear children for self enhancement and use hostility against their mothers to deprive themselves of an achieving, successful, and happy life are indications that some of the respondents support the low self esteem trait in the culture of poverty.

Suggested Agenda to the Culture of Poverty

The findings of this study also suggest additions to the Culture of Poverty model on the subculture level. Hence, they suggest that the universal norm of legitimacy exists among black single mothers in Tidewater. Also, the findings indicate that sex and pregnancy among teens are highly related to school activities and school vacation; therefore, seasonal pregnancies are a characteristic feature of the culture of poverty among teens. Not only do the Tidewater findings suggest an addition to the culture of poverty, on the subculture level, from the perspective of schools, but also from the perspective of churches. Hence, it is indicated that church leaders enhance sex participation and pregnancy among young church girls.

The findings in this study also suggest additions to family traits in the culture of poverty. They are inadequate, early, ongoing mother-daughter talk about pregnancy, single parenthood, and its expensive, lonely, and burdensome nature, mother permissiveness -- childhood freedom -- and grandmother's encouragement to their daughters to become mothers more than once through assistance with childrearing, housing, and financial support. Also, male neighbors, boyfriends, and householders' -- mothers' boyfriends', stepfathers', fathers', uncles', and cousins' participation in sex with young girls in the home is a useful trait to the family level of the poverty. As a response to these traits, black female sex and menstrual power is described and advocated for black unmarrieds (See Chapter Eight).

Self-Correcting Poverty

Also, some single mothers realize self-correcting poverty. Hence, they were mainly employed women and six mothers were employed as managers and officials.

CHAPTER FOUR

SINGLE MOTHERHOOD

Introduction

The findings in Chapter Two and Three, existing research, and new knowledge about single parenthood led to our 1986 research among single mothers and fathers in Norfolk, Virginia. Starting with sex education in the home, this chapter describes the history of single motherhood, analyzes the findings, and relates them to Malinowski's Principle of Legitimacy. Also, it relates the findings to Oscar Lewis' Culture of Poverty theory, and suggests addenda and a Self-Correcting poverty proposition.

Method

This chapter is about single non-college mothers in Norfolk, Virginia. It is based on interviews and autobiographies obtained from black, single mothers during the spring and summer, in 1986, supplemented by observation information. Using an interview schedule, each mother was asked questions about several factors, including socioeconomic status, number of children, age and location of first sex experience, and age of first sex partner. Subsequently the oral history of each respondent was obtained by using a preconstructed format, designed as the second part of the interview schedule; the procedure provided consistency in data collection. Rather than using a tape recorder, responses were handwritten and sometimes checked by respondents. In general, this method is modeled after the work of Oscar Lewis. For example, in Five Families (1959), The Children of Sanchez (1961), and La Vida, 1965), Lewis used the family as the unit of study; and developed the Culture of Poverty theory on the subculture, family and individual level. In The Children of Sanchez and La Vida, family members tell their own life stories in their own words. Lewis found autobiographies a useful approach in studying lower-class Mexican life and Puerto Rican family

48

life (1965:xix). What we found in Norfolk is that the respondents are greatly aware of their circumstances and, therefore, found it easy to relate their stories.

Our study was designed to examine the background of single mothers, their interpersonal relations with the fathers of their children, with their mothers, with their children, and with the mothers of the fathers of their children, what they would do in retrospect, and the relevance of the Culture of Poverty model to single motherhood in Norfolk, Virginia. Results of this research indicate varied patterns in each aspect of single motherhood. Starting with their background, eight of the twenty-nine respondents grew up in two parent households. Further nineteen respondents were mothers only once while ten were mothers twice or more. Their background also indicates that after the onset of motherhood, some respondents discontinued their education while others are correcting its impact. Their interpersonal relations with their families, the fathers of their children, and the mothers of the fathers of their children, were similarly varied. From the perspective of the fathers of their children, the respondents' love relationship ranged from none to a relatively strong emotional bond; likewise, some of the respondents loved the fathers of their children less after than before the onset of pregnancy while others loved them more and still others did not realize a change. However in general the respondents gave the fathers of their children more love than they received. Also, concerning romantic feelings, there was varied behavior. For example, during pregnancy, some respondents were less interested in sex while others' romantic feelings remained unchanged; and a third pattern was they increased. Unlike love and romantic feelings, the respondents, except for a few, did not experience an economic relationship with the fathers of their children. Hence, becoming a mother is not equated with material gifts and economic support. In fact, the economic experience between the respondents and the fathers of their children centers around child support. Even so, there is variation; a few respondents receive a definite amount of child support at specified times while others receive either inadequate support at unspecified times or no child support.

The respondents also experience varied interpersonal relations on the consanguineal and fictive affinal level. Specifically, on the consanguineal level, they experience work, responsibility, and joy while interacting with their children; on the other hand, with their mothers, they experience warm normal and strained difficult relations. Similarly, with a group of fictive affines, their boyfriends' mothers, the respondents experience an absence of relations, along with strained, helping, and close relationships. In addition, all the respondents except three indicated that if they knew what they know now and could live their lives over, they would not become single parents.

Respondents' Background

<u>Age and Education</u>

The sample is comprised of twenty-nine single mothers in Norfolk, Virginia (See Chapter Seven, Table 1). The respondents range in age from sixteen years to over forty; however, eight are between age sixteen and nineteen.

No one's education was limited to elementary school; two had achieved some junior high school training while thirteen had achieved between ten and twele years of schooling, nine had graduated from high school, and five had obtained one to three years of college training. Twenty of the respondents were not working; of the remaining nine, one each was a clerk, cook, custodian, Southeastern Tidewater Opportunity Project (STOP) trainee, cashier, fast food employee, teacher assistant, factory worker, and index clerk. Though we did not always ask about source of income, of the twenty-two asked, nine reported they work while thirteen noted they receive assistance from Aid to Dependent Children (ADC) and Women, Infants, and Children (WIC), an indication that the respondents experience a shortage of cash soon after receipt of employment or public assistance checks.

A more detailed analysis of the respondents' education and work data indicate a self-correcting process. Although, during pregnancy, a majority discontinued their education, eleven respondents are correcting or have somewhat corrected the interruption of their education. Even though they have not eliminated poverty in their lives, they are improving one element -- education. Our premise is that there is an inverse relationship between high education and poverty. The eleven respondents who corrected or lessened the impact of single parenthood on their educational achievement described themselves thusly:

> I am seventeen years old and became a mother in August 1986. In September, I shall return to the Coronado Vocational School and graduate in the spring. When motherhood set in, rather than stop school, because of embarrassment, I transfered to the vocational-tech school last year. I remained on the honor roll all year and won several awards; second place award in fashion designing, three awards in catering, one Gold Medal in catering, first place ribbon in catering, and third place ribbon in catering.

> I am sixteen years old and had my baby at age sixteen. I have already made arrangements with my family to return to school in September 1986.

> Now I am nineteen, but I had my baby at age eighteen. It was necessary to stop school a while. In September, I will return to school in the eleventh grade and stay in school until I graduate.

> I became a mother at age seventeen. Now I am eighteen, in the twelfth grade, and my baby is five months old. I will return to high school in September, graduate next spring, and enroll at Norfolk State University in the fall. I attended school the whole time I was pregnant and passed my school work. That puts me in the right grade.

> I am now eighteen and became a mother at age seventeen. Because I dropped out of school, I have not finished the eleventh grade. This September I will return to school and complete the eleventh grade. The next year I will graduate. I am happy that Mama agreed to keep the baby so that I can go back to school.

> I was lucky! I had my baby at age seventeen, remained in school, while I was pregnant, and completed the eleventh grade. I will return to school in September, complete the twelfth grade and graduate.

> I am now twenty-three years old. I became a mother at seventeen. After the baby was born, I went back to high school and graduated.

Even though I had my baby at nineteen, I decided to continue my education. After two and a half years of college, I became an index clerk. I am overworked and underpaid, but I will keep this job until I find one that matches my skills and pays proper wages. My income is supplemented by welfare assistance and I don't like welfare.

The latter mother indicates self-correcting behavior in education, employment, and, hopefully, wages. A similar example is a twenty-seven year old respondent who became a mother at age twenty-four. Because she wanted to do more than receive welfare, she became a teacher assistant. Likewise, a thirty-eight year old respondent became a mother at age eighteen, yet she completed high school and attended Tidewater Community College two years; a thirty-one year old respondent became a mother at eighteen and is attempting to correct her employment status in a STOP training program. These findings indicate that eleven respondents are correcting their poverty situation by increasing their education, obtaining a job, and desiring better wages.

Sex

We also inquired about the origin of the respondents' sex activity (See Chapter Seven, Table 1). Hence, we asked how old they were at the time of their first sex experience. As indicated in their responses, they began sex life between twelve and nineteen with sixteen saying between twelve and sixteen years of age and thirteen between seventeen and nineteen. Compared to respondents, as shown in Table 1, first sex partners were somewhat older; five were between twelve and sixteen years old while twenty-three were seventeen to twenty-eight. In effect, the women were often first introduced to sex by males older than themselves. Moreover, the women destroyed the myth that one cannot get pregnant the first time she engages in sex. Though our data are not complete on this question, we documented that two respondents reported they became pregnant the first time they engaged in sex. Also, near the end of the research process, we discovered the location of their first sex experience. Of the eleven respondents asked this question, two reported that it occurred in a hotel, two noted their boyfriends' apartments, six their boyfriends' mothers' homes, and one noted her home. According to this respondent, she and her boyfriend utilized her bedroom with maternal consent. Similarly, another respondent noted, "My boyfriend's mother ran that kind of house"; for a small fee, a room could be rented. Nevertheless, the significant finding is that, of the eleven respondents, queried, eight engaged in sex the first time at their boyfriend's apartment or his parents' home.

First Pregnancy

Once we understood the respondents' first sexual experience. we also wanted to know about their first pregnancy. As indicated in Chapter Seven, Table 1, of twenty-eight responding, twenty were between sixteen and nineteen years of age when they had their first child while eight were between age twenty and twenty-four. Attempting to get a feel for the emotional setting, in which the children were conceived, we found that eighteen respondents became mothers of children by their favorite boyfriends while six indicated the men were not their favorite boyfriends. Even so, only eight respondents wanted their first child at the time of conception while thirteen boyfriends were favorable toward becoming parents. Seven of the respondents were from single parent homes; hence, there is evidence of self-perpetuating and non-perpetuating poverty.

Motherhood and Fatherhood One or More Times

Because there has also been concern about black women bearing children one or more times, we determined the number of children per mother and found that fifteen women had one child or were expecting their first child, and fourteen were single mothers twice or more (See Chapter Seven, Table 1). Hence, the sample is almost evenly divided between the women who are mothers only once and the women who are mothers twice or more. As also noted in Chapter Seven, Table 1, ten of the women mothered children by two or three fathers. Hence, our findings suggest yet another pattern among the respondents who are mothers twice or more; they became mothers for more than one father. When the same woman bears children by more than one man, this seems to diminish the relevance of both men. In fact, birth of a child by a second or third father seems to have the potential of relieving at least the first father of his responsibilities. Because of single parenthood, because some respondents are mothers twice or more, because some respondents' children are fathered by two or more men, we determined to understand single motherhood by focusing on the nature of single mothers' relationships.

Interpersonal Relationships

Respondents and Their Parents

This analysis of interpersonal relations is begun with childhood relations between the respondents and their mothers. We thus determined the type of girl talk between the respondents and their mothers. We asked them what their mothers had told them about boys and sex before their first sex experience. Answers fit three response categories; one group of eleven respondents had not experienced mother-daughter talk. Of these women, one said, "My mother didn't tell me anything about sex. She was very strict. My parents were very religious; for example, my father was a deacon and my mother was one of the mothers (deeply religious and respected women) of our church." Seven other respondents comprise a second group whose mothers had mentioned sex to them. They had not been told much, however, because their mothers were shy, or they were raised by their grandmothers. On the other hand, twelve other respondents, the third response group, had experienced mother-daughter talk before engaging in sex. For example, one respondent's mother had told her, at the time of first menses, "You know you can get pregnant now." Another respondent's mother's usual expression in discussions about sex was , "Don't play with fire." The remaining mothers told their daughters to let them know when they were ready for birth control, emphasized its use in sex life, and one explained the consequences.

Given the somewhat limited mother-daughter talk about sex and boys, we determined their relationship after the onset of pregnancy. One mother-daughter pattern of interaction was warmth. For example, a mother "was happy that her baby was having a baby," another was glad, while a third mother was happy and advised the respondent against an abortion. This case is an example of authoritarianism described in the family of the poor (Lewis 1966). Similarly, three grandmothers who reared the respondents were happy. A respondent noted,

"It was my grandmother's first great grandchild and she was happy and did not want me to work" while another grandmother was happy because she was an only child and wanted a grandchild; still another grandmother, according to the respondent, was happy, though she did not say anything. It could be that favorable responses from grandmothers and great grandmothers to single parenthood lead to single or even multiple births outside marriage.

According to two additional respondents, another pattern of mother and daughter behavior was normal relations. For example, in one case, the respondent's daddy was off work the day she told her mother and they were the same as usual; similarly, in the second case, the mother was calm and talked with her daughter. Three other respondents and their mothers experienced strained behavior; hence, one mother was "kind of disappointed" while another replied, "I told you so." On the other hand, eight respondents and their mothers experienced difficult relations. According to the respondents, they were either "upset" or "angry." For example, one respondent noted:

> My boyfriend told my mama to sit down because he wanted to talk with us. Mama was very upset and wanted to see what he had planned. He wanted to marry me and still does, however, I thought I was too young. Because I have his baby, doesn't mean I want to live with him the rest of my life. We are close and sometimes I enjoy sex with him.

This finding seems to suggest that parenthood is equated with neither happiness nor marriage. Hence, one task is to see that young people recognize that only marriage licenses parenthood (Malinowski 1966:37). Another respondent related, "Mama was upset because she wanted at least one of her six children to finish college and she was depending on me." Hence, this respondent's mother found her daughter's single motherhood a traumatic experience because she expected uninterrupted success that would give her daughter the good life -- education, a good job, and good wages. This finding is supported by Shimkin (1978:122) and Bernard (1966:52-55) who observed that out of wedlock births in some low income families are a traumatic experience.

The Respondents and the Mothers of Their Boyfriends

Much as motherhood fosters new mother-daughter relations, it sometimes restructures relations between single mothers and the mothers of the fathers of their children. Though ten respondents were not asked about their relationships with the mothers of their boyfriends, of the ones asked, seven reported there is no relationship while eleven reported several patterns. One pattern is closeness; hence, three respondents reported they are very close or close to the mothers of the fathers of their children. Three other women noted a helping relationship between the mothers of the fathers of their children and themselves. For example, one respondent replied,"I have a relationship with her. When I need her, she tries to help me. She visits me and I take the baby to see her. She has ten children and the father of my child is the first one to graduate from college," and "We are not close, but she is nice toward us. She will help, if needed, with baby sitting." Several other respondents described the relationship between them and the mothers of the fathers of their children as strained. They described it in such terms as "I don't have any dealings with her because his family and I don't get along," "I can't stand my boyfriend's mother because she has a nasty attitude," and "I don't communicate with them."

The Respondents and the Fathers of Their Children

The way single motherhood restructures behavior is even more vivid in interpersonal relations between the respondents and the fathers of their children. We began this inquiry by asking the respondents whether they and the fathers and their children discussed certain questions prior to the onset of pregnancy. For example, we asked whether they had discussed what they would do if they became parents, how the child would be supported, what life would be like with a child, and what they wanted out of life. We found that only five respondents had discussed the situation with their boyfriends. Before pregnancy, three planned marriage and another respondent and her boyfriend had decided to become parents and then get jobs. Girlfriend-boyfriend talk about the consequences of sex was limited like mother-daughter talk.

Although some mothers of the respondents had not discussed contraception in girl talk, although couples had not paid much attention to possible pregnancy and its consequences, we asked the respondents whether they were using birth control at the time of pregnancy. Except for two women, neither the respondents nor their boyfriends were using birth control when pregnancy occurred. What this means, according to respondents, is that they had the pill, but had missed taking it one day, a couple of days, or had discontinued its use. It was discontinued, because the pill caused headaches, dizziness, weight gain, or vomiting. For example, one respondent noted:

> I was on birth control pills. First the doctor gave me white ones, then he gave me pink ones. Because they made me sick on the stomach and I vomited blood, I stopped taking them. The doctor said there was nothing wrong with the pills and the last time I reported my problem, he told me to stop taking them; five or six months later, I became pregnant.

According to the respondent, if she had been given a pill that agreed with her body, she would not have become pregnant. In still another case, a respondent noted:

> I used the pill until it ran out; because my menses came three times a month, the doctor told me I could not take any more. After my third child, he said he tied my tubes, yet I had the fourth baby. His response was, 'You know they can come loose,' however, the second time he tied, clipped, and burned them. According to my doctor, when a women menstruates a great deal, even though her tubes are tied, she can get pregnant."

It appears that both respondents could have prevented pregnancy by using a back-up contraceptive.

After learning that the respondents had not regularly practiced birth control, two excepted, we asked why they engaged in sex and took a chance on becoming pregnant. The women gave varied reasons for risking pregnancy. For example, one woman became pregnant because her boyfriend told her he was using condoms, but he deceived her. Another became pregnant because she was raped. On the other hand, three other respondents noted that an overpowering sex desire led to their pregnancy.

In other cases, the respondents became mothers because of peer pressure. One of these mothers noted, "Because other girls were having children, I just wanted a child. Though my baby is only five months old, the father of my child and I do not court anymore because we had problems; both of us have a nasty attitude, and I can't get along with him." Then some of the respondents became mothers, because they liked the man so much, wanted a baby by him, or wanted to honor his request for a baby. Both findings, peer pressure and desire to satisfy boyfriends, suggest that some black women love their men better than themselves.

After learning why the respondents chanced motherhood and the way it was decided, we asked them to describe their first reaction upon learning they were expecting their first child. Again, we found several patterns, including happiness. Though five women did not respond to this question, seven noted they were happy, and used such words as "happy," "excited," and "serious tripping" to identify more clearly their feelings. Of course, one added that she was happy because she had no other choice while another related she was happy because it was her first child. A second pattern was that six respondents had mixed emotions about becoming pregnant. They were surprised, happy, and determined to give their children a good life. Simultaneously, they were angry, didn't believe in abortions, scared more so than glad, and fluctuated between happiness and sadness; beside, they were confused and were not sure they desired a baby.

However, the largest number of respondents, ten, demonstrated a third pattern, unhappiness. They were unhappy about becoming pregnant and expressed surprise, shock, and fear of motherhood. They were also, according to them, "sad," "mad," "evil," "upset," "determined to finish high school -- no matter what -- and go to college." They also cried, felt alone, and had a sense of disappointment.

It is apparent that poor black single mothers in our Norfolk sample responded variously to news of their forthcoming motherhood. Another important pattern is that of twenty-three respondents, only a minority was happy.

Next, we turned to the economic support of children. We asked the respondents how much and now often the fathers of their children give child support. There were three response patterns. Eighteen men provide no support. In a second category, eight respondents gave vague responses that precluded understanding it. Unlike this category, in the third group, three respondents were very clear about the support the fathers of their children provide. For example, a respondent with a one year old girl receives $120 monthly and the father buys the child material gifts while another mother of one child receives $150.00 bimonthly. And a respondent with a boy and girl, by the same father, receives $400.00 a month. Hence, regular and specific amounts of economic child support are given to only a few respondents by the fathers of their children. The major patterns are that respondents either receive inadequate support, at unspecified times, or no support; hence, in general, child support is fragile and unreliable.

After we determined child support, we continued to learn how respondents' boyfriends demonstrated love to their children. We found a number of patterns, including daily fatherly love. That is, there are men who see their children on a daily basis, give presents, bathe them, and take them places. The next pattern consists of weekend fathers who take their children to their homes for weekends, tell them they are loved, and have private talks. One mother who responded this way noted that the father of her child gets paid Fridays and takes her and the baby shopping Saturdays. An unusual respondent, with a weekend arrangement, is a girl who was disappointed with her pregnancy by her college boyfriend who attends a prestigious university. However, as she put it, after the baby was born, she came to her sense, resumed courtship, and obtained his engagement ring. When he graduates in May 1987, they will get married and he will send her to secretarial school. If this mother's plans materialize, she will not only demonstrate self-correcting education, but she is likely to become a middle income mother in a nuclear family. In still another case, we see a different pattern, the respondent's boyfriend takes care of the child by him as well as those fathered by other men.

Upon learning that fathers of the respondents' children give the children more love than economic support, our next concern focused on ways fathers show the respondents love. Initial inspection of love relationships indicated two types. One pattern is love discontinuity. That is, the men, the women say, are not loving toward them and do not communicate; nor do the men come to see them.

The second pattern, according to nineteen respondents, is loving relationships. What we found is that loving relationships also vary. One such pattern is child help and child support; the women consider it love for themselves if fathers take care of their children daily or weekends and provide economic support. In these relationships, the emotional bond is not described as an element in love behavior; thus, motherhood greatly deprives these respondents of previous emotional bonding with the fathers of their children. This pattern is sometimes initiated as soon as a man learns he is becoming a father. However, it often begins shortly after the birth of the child. A second variation of the love pattern, among five women with children by more than one man, finds one of the men demonstrating love, but not the others. For example, the first father left a respondent; after pregnancy, the second father of her children went back to his wife, but the third father supports and helps her with her three children. A third variation of loving relationships is that respondents see their boyfriends and engage in arguments or otherwise share each other's presence. What seems important is that respondents still have the opportunity to see the fathers of their children, which is not always available to single mothers. A fourth type of loving relationship is that the men give the respondents hugs and kisses and material gifts, but not sex. On the other hand, six of the women indicated still a fifth type of loving relationship -- the fathers of their children show them love. Five of these women had one child, except one respondent with two children. The last woman said both men are lovely, except that the second does not show his child love. These women's boyfriends show love by hugging and kissing them, saying they love them (though not often enough), sharing material gifts, and reacting warmly toward them. As one respondent stated, "He loves me, tells me so, and gave me an engagement ring." According to the respondents, two patterns, lack of love and love support characterize their lives; also, the love experience varies widely among the respondents. As shown, love for respondents can mean total lack of emotional expression to warm, though inadequate, bonding.

Another important aspect of emotional bonding between single mothers and the fathers of their children concerns the love they manifest to the fathers of their first child. Starting with pregnancy, we found several variations. For example, four respondents loved their boyfriends less after than before pregnancy, because they went through mental changes, were angry about pregnancy, and pregnancy interfered with their freedom. On the other hand, six of the respondents related there was no change in the love they had for the fathers of their children. Unlike these respondents, twelve others indicated they loved their boyfriends more after they conceived their child than before. The respondents' love was stronger because their boyfriends supported them during pregnancy and gave them more attention than previously received. Also, the respondents noted that it made them feel good to carry his baby, have a part of him inside her, carry something in her they shared, and possess something of his.

There were still two others patterns among a few of the women who had children by more than one father. One women loved the first boyfriend more, but the other two less, while another respondent loved the first boyfriend less, loved the second a lot, but he was married, and loved the third most because he supported her. In general the respondents loved the fathers of their children more than the men loved them.

To further clarify the respondents' love for the fathers of their children, we determined their sexual/romantic feelings after learning they were expecting their first child. Their love feelings were varied. For example, some of the women were less interested in sex, because they had no desire, were upset, felt funny being pregnant, or didn't feel like engaging in sex. Moreover, one respondent did not desire sex because she was looking for more out of what her parents had given her than pregnancy and the type of boyfriend who fathered her child; that is, she appeared to feel that her relatively good family background qualified her for a more successful man than the father of her child. The second pattern was that romantic/sexual feelings remained unchanged while the third pattern, experienced by one respondent, shows that the woman did not have sex with the first two fathers, but her desire increased with the third father who continues to support her economically. In some cases, romantic feelings are linked to degree of economic support. Also, seven respondents described a fourth pattern which was increased sexual/romantic feelings because they no longer had reason to fear pregnancy.

Whether the women find single motherhood an enormous responsibility, or enjoy motherhood and, in general, the fathers of their children, we asked why they did not marry the fathers of their first child. According to the respondents, there are several reasons. For example, one respondent noted, "I don't want to marry him because I don't want to marry anybody now. If he askes me, I probably will. I would only marry him." Another said, "Neither of us wanted marriage." Still another mother noted, "He was not ready for it and my father got a shotgun, meaning he tried to make the young man marry me." Furthermore, a few respondents related they did not want to get married; for example, one mother noted, "The first father was already married and I didn't think the second father would be a good choice" while another related, "I wasn't ready because I was too young and didn't want the responsibility" and still another noted, "He acted too stupid and was older." Five other respondents gave these as reasons for not marrying the fathers of their children: "I did not want to marry him because I wanted to be free. I don't know who will come around. Perhaps I will marry around age forty so I will have plenty of time to meet other men and have fun," "He asked me, but my grandmother will not sign the papers," "I was raped," "He asked me to marry him, but I refused because I was young and disturbed. He had just started working and we did not know how his job would turn out," and "With the first father, I was too young and he was no good; the second father was married; and the third father and I are going to get married."

The Respondents and Their Children

Whether the respondents and the fathers of their children experienced a strong emotional bond, we determined the meaning of motherhood to the respondents. A response was that motherhood involves a lot of responsibility. For example, a few responded, "It means a lot of time toward the baby and there is no time for anything but my baby" and "It is a tremendous responsibility and lots of hard work." Another response bespeaks the joy of single motherhood. For example, a respondent replied, "It gives me someone with whom to spend time" while another replied, "It's priceless. I think the world of my daughter. I like teaching her new things, including sentence construction. There are times when she takes me to the last notch; yet, she also says things creatively and sweet. I would not let anything take the place of her."

In Retrospect

Since a majority of respondents either had mixed emotions or regrets about becoming mothers the first time, since some respondents noted their desire and happiness about pregnancy and motherhood, since some find motherhood enormous responsibility, since some respondents experience stress in relations with their mothers and the mothers of the fathers of their children, since none married the father of their children, it seemed necessary to determine whether the respondents loved their children because they had them but really preferred not to be mothers. This, to us, appeared to be the supreme test of our people's interest in bearing children out of wedlock. Therefore, we asked, If you could live your life over and know what you know now, would you live it the same way?

All the respondents, except three, indicated that if they knew what they know now and could live their lives over, they would live differently, as described in their own comments. One respondent, for example, noted:

> "I was a star basketball player in high school. I played forward and point guard. My goals were to finish high school and go to college four years and play basketball in college. I always made Bs and Cs and athletes were required to make at least a C average to stay on the team. Now I plan to finish high school and get a good job. If I had known what I know now, I would have waited to have a baby."

The remainder of the respondents gave similar responses such as, "I would be married and plan my motherhood," "I wouldn't have a child; instead, I would go to college and get a good job. To prevent motherhood, I would stay on the pill or use some kind of birth control," and "I wish I had listened to my parents," along with "I probably would change because I don't want to be on welfare the rest of my life -- they are too strict."

The theme of their responses was repeated many times by addditional respondents who said "I would earn my high school diploma, get a nice job, and marry before having a child. I would use birth control to keep from getting pregnant, and I wouldn't get pregnant because I would stay on the pill." Another respondent lamented, "I would do something altogether different. My father worked at LaGuardia Airport and wanted me to become an airline stewardess. Had I done what he wanted, life would be different." Then, another respondent established her priorities thusly: "First, I would get an education; second, I would become financially stable; and third, I would get married and have children" while another thought in terms of life being twice as good as single motherhood; she said, "I wouldn't have any children. I would finish high school, perhaps go to college, and then get an apartment. Life would be 100 percent better than it is now. Birth control was the answer." Perhaps the most drastic change is expressed by the respondent who noted, "I wouldn't have children. I would get my tubes tied. I wouldn't have sex, because it brings babies, unless I was married."

These responses seem to support the observation that there is a difference between loving a child, because one is its mother, and evaluating motherhood, after the experience, as one's desired status. The responses, in the words of the single mothers, clearly indicate there is a difference. They also suggest a need for a stronger pre-pregnancy awareness program, in the Norfolk housing developments, to thoroughly alert girls to what lies ahead in one's relationship with a young man and their parents and his parents, as well as what happens to one's own goals and aspirations, when one becomes a mother too early, coupled with the disadvantages of single parenthood. Moreover, though poor, the women's views in retrospect indicate that, before pregnancy, they had hope and aspirations.

Discussion

An attempt has been made to place the analysis of single motherhood, in Norfolk, Virginia, in the context of the samples characteristics, interpersonal relations and economic support patterns, and retrospection. Starting with their educational and employment characteristics, after the onset of motherhood, some respondents discontinued their education; however, eleven are in the process of correcting the impact of motherhood on their education. Next, the single mothers experienced multiple patterns of interpersonal relations with their families, fathers of their children, and the mothers of the fathers of their children. Also, while making the transition from childhood to young adulthood, they experienced sex interaction and child-bearing (20 mothers). However, the women's boyfriends, more often than themselves, preferred single parenthood. Furthermore, in the context of relationships in general, the respondents experienced a low level of interaction with their parents about birth control and with their boyfriends about using contraception, risking pregnancy, and what their lives would be like, if they conceived. On the other hand, a high level of interaction occurred with peers, which contributed to childbearing.

Though eight respondents grew up in single parent homes, fourteen were mothers more than once, and ten experienced childbearing for more than one man. Sex interaction led to another type of interpersonal behavior, reactions to becoming single mothers. With their boyfriends and family, they interacted several ways. Hence, they were variously happy, uncertain about their desire to become mothers, or happy about the event.

Still other varied patterns of interpersonal behavior were evident in the love relationships between the respondents and the fathers of their children. The love shown the respondents ranged from none to a relatively strong emotional bond; similarly, some of the respondents loved the fathers of their children less after then before the onset of pregnancy while others loved them more and still others did not realize a change. Also, concerning romantic feelings, there was varied interpersonal behavior. Hence, during pregnancy, some respondents were less interested in sex while others' romantic feelings remained unchanged; and a third pattern was that they increased. Even so, the respondents did not usually desire marriage to the fathers of their first child. The reasons include the respondents' beliefs that the men were not good choices for husbands, they did not want to sacrifice their freedom, the men did not desire marriage, and the unavailability of a father.

Therefore, the respondents experienced varied interpersonal relations on the consanguineal and fictive affinal level. Specifically, on the consanguineal level, they experienced work, responsibility, and joy while interacting with their children; on the other hand, with their mothers, they experienced warm normal and strained difficult relations. Similarly, with a group of fictive affines, their boyfriends' mothers, the respondents experienced an absence of relations, along with strained, helping, and close relationships.

Turning next to spending patterns, we noted the fathers' child support. The major patterns are inadequate support at indefinite times or no support at all; hence, financial support was fragile and unreliable. Therefore, either the women mothered children by men who were unable to support them or the men made other choices for spending money.

The Culture of Poverty Model

Our second task in this essay concerns the "Culture of Poverty" model. Initially, we placed the single motherhood analysis in the context of the culture of poverty. It is concluded that the Norfolk, black, single mothers support the model on the subculture-societal, communal, family, and individual levels (See Chapter Seven, Table 2). The traits and their indicators that support each level of the Culture of Poverty model are summarized in this table. Hence, we concluded that the model is useful for understanding single motherhood among the Norfolk, black, poor.

Suggested Traits for Broadening the Culture of Poverty Model

Also, because of additional findings, we suggest some previously unreported traits for the model. For example, on the communal level, we suggest that single mothers' social contacts are confined to their courtyards and nearby courtyards, friends' homes, stores, and the street (various places of entertainment). Moreover, judging by the establishment of Young and Calvert Parks, as public housing developments, in the fifties, it also appears that there is communal intergenerational perpetuation of poverty sites.

On the family level of the Culture of Poverty model, we also recommend traits found in our Norfolk study that as far as we can determine have not been reported. They include a low level of communication with the fathers of their children before the onset of parenthood about their futures. Also, we recommend for the family level of the model, as indicated by eight respondents, intrapersonal perpetuation of motherhood more than once along with intrapersonal perpetuation of motherhood by more than one father. Beside, on the individual level, we suggest several traits, including enhancement of love for boyfriends during pregnancy because the respondents had a part of the men inside them, the respondents developed a sense of love through child support, and they honored their boyfriends' request for a baby and in general, as a result of compliance, they lost their boyfriends' love.

Next, we place our single motherhood analysis in the context of a recommended Self-Correcting Poverty proposition.

Self-Correcting Poverty Proposition

Beside providing support for the Culture of Poverty model and providing additional traits on the community, family, and individual level, on the basis of other questions raised in our study and some new findings, we suggest that self-correcting poverty coexists with self-perpetuating poverty. The specific indications of self-correcting poverty are noted in Chapter Seven, Table 3. For example, one new finding concerns the retrospective belief system of the respondents in this study and in my study of unwed college fathers and mothers at Norfolk State University; another new finding is that 38 percent (11) of the respondents are correcting the impact of motherhood on their educational achievement. With improved education, it is likely that other aspects of poverty will be self-correcting. Hence, we suggest solid education as an intervention strategy for all males and females in housing developments. Both new findings indicate that the respondents do not want to be part of the Other Americans (Harrington 1962) nor do they desire to continue the perpetuation of poverty (Lewis 1965; Moynihan 1967, Clark 1965) and single parenthood (Clark 1965); hence, some black, poor, single mothers are hopeful. Even among the single mothers in this study, who have not started over, their desire to possess a different status from their current circumstances indicates that, with proper social machinery -- solid education, sex and pregnancy prevention education, good jobs, hard work, enhanced self image, and encouragement -- their own lives could become self-correcting.

Another reason we recommend a self-correcting poverty proposition is that, among twenty-nine single mothers, in the same urban poverty setting, we are unable to generalize their behavior. Instead, in depth analysis revealed multiple patterns in their personal characteristics and interpersonal relations. Hence, this essay, with one exception, supports the literature of the seventies. The exception is that our findings bring together, in the same study, both ideological positions regarding the culture of poverty. Hence, we conclude that self-correcting poverty as well as self-perpetuating poverty coexist in the same poor conditions.

Moreover, like Oscar Lewis, we also contend that there is one western subculture of poverty; however, unlike Lewis, we suggest that some characteristics dominate specific cultures while other characteristics dominate still other cultures; yet, the specific cultures possess common traits, including poor education and low paying jobs. Beside, our findings do not suggest a vivid division along class lines. That is, because we found self-correcting and self-perpetuating poverty in the same settings, we postulate similarities between class cultures. If our reasoning is accurate, we will find some poor using other classes as behavior models. We have some verification for this observation. For example, overlapping characteristics were found among black beauty parlors by social class in Newport News, Virginia (Barnes 1975:15) and among black Protestant congregations in Atlanta, Georgia, yet distinct denominations exist (Barnes 1985:40-49); hence, we expect overlapping characteristics between the poor and non-poor as well as self-correcting and self-perpetuating poverty in western, urban, black, single parent communities.

What our suggested self-correcting poverty proposition also entails is raising the kinds of questions we researched, as well as others, including the roles of grandmothers and great grandmothers in the single parenthood complex, and taking a critical look at the application of the Culture of Poverty model to large populations, to use this important model to describe poverty and determine additional traits as well as other traits for the recommended self-correcting poverty proposition, as it applies to urban, black women and men everywhere, especially, western, urban, poor, black, single mothers.

An earlier version of this chapter was presented in the Symposium, "Women in the Americas: Relationships, Work, and Power," at the Eighty Fifth Annual Meeting of the American Anthropological Association, Philadelphia, Pennsylvania, December 1986.

CHAPTER FIVE

SINGLE FATHERHOOD

Introduction

As noted in Chapter One, very little attention has been paid black, single fathers. In an attempt to broaden our understanding of single parenthood, this chapter analyzes the behavior of black single fathers who either have not completed high school or college. Our specific aims are to describe the history of single fatherhood, discuss the findings, relate them to Malinowski's Principle of Legitimacy and Oscar Lewis' Culture of Poverty model as well as modify the model. Our findings indicate self-correcting behavior on the subculture, family, and individual level. Hence, we concluded that simultaneously with selfperpetuating poverty there is self-correction taking place in the same setting. With the reversal of poverty in process, it is likely that it will spread to more black, single males and therefore lessen poverty among blacks. Also, to enhance the self-correcting process, as shown in Chapter Eight, our findings are used to develop pregnancy prevention models. As we noted in Chapter four, in our opinion, elimination of single parenthood will lead to self-correcting poverty. Because a majority of people desire the good life, we believe that single blacks will respond to implementation of the data-based models.

Also this chapter examines single fatherhood from several perspectives. Therefore emphasis is placed on background characteristics of the respondents, their interpersonal relationships with the mothers of the children, why they did not marry the first mother of their children, their economic and emotional relations with their children, the meaning of fatherhood, reactions of their mothers to their fatherhood, and what they would do in retrospect.

Another dimension of this chapter concerns female roles in the respondents' sex life, preventive sex education, violation of sex norms, and results, derivatives from single fatherhood, and fatherhood prevention.

Still another dimension of this chapter is the determination of the relevance of the findings to additional questions central to the literature of the black family. Hence, we asked, Do the respondents in Norfolk and Tidewater, Virginia support Malinowski's Principle of Legitimacy? Do they support Oscar Lewis' Culture of Poverty? Do the respondents provide information that indicates the culture of poverty should be expanded? Do the respondents provide data that suggest the need to modify the Culture of Poverty model?

Method

During the spring and summer of 1986, Jeanne Clarke, Shelcie Moss, and I interviewed nineteen single fathers in Young Park and Calvert Park, subsidized housing developments in Norfolk, Virginia; however, two respondents are residents of Suffolk, a nearby town. The same methods, structured interviews and oral history formats, were used to obtain data as were used with single mothers described in Chapter Four.

Respondents' Background

Age, Education, Occupation and Income

The respondents vary widely among themselves in age, education, occupation, income, birth status, and first sex experience. Regarding age, the single fathers range between fifteen and thirty years of age. Two were teens, nine were between twenty and twenty-four, three were between twenty-five and twenty-nine, four were thirty or over, and one did not give his age. However, when the respondents fathered their first child, eleven were teens, fifteen to nineteen years of age, six were twenty to twenty-four, and one was twenty-five.

The respondents' education ranged from junior high school to three and a half years of college. Hence, four attended college, one attended vocational school, nine graduated from high school, thirteen discontinued their education between the tenth and twelfth grade, and one each discontinued junior high school in the seventh and ninth grade. Their training, for the most part, has equipped them for blue collar employment. Though six of the respondents are unemployed, one each is employed in roofing, truck driving, navy security, construction, fork lift driving, the shipyard, painting, and maintenance. On the other hand, two are in sales work and three are in food services. Seven of the men gave their monthly earnings; two earn between $400 and $900 monthly, two others earn between $1400 and $1500, one earns $1200, and two earn respectively $2700 and $3000 monthly.

Birth Status

At birth, twelve respondents were born to married parents while six were children of single parents, and one respondent did not note his birth status.

First Sex Experience

Because a great deal has been written about the early sex life of black youth, we asked the respondents how old they and the girls were at the time of their first sex experience. We found that eighteen were between five and seventeen years of age and one was twenty-one; however, twelve experienced sex at age thirteen. Overall, five respondents shared their first experience with girls their age, six with younger girls, and eight with older girls.

Among seventeen of the respondents, eight initiated their first sex experience while four respondents and their girlfriends decided to engage in sex. On the other hand, a respondent's girlfriend initiated his experience while baby sitters initiated the first sex experience in the lives of three respondents; in another case, a teenager taught his sister and a respondent how to have sex.

Fatherly Context

The respondents also vary widely among themselves in number of children fathered, number of women who birthed them, and desire for children. Hence, we found that ten respondents fathered one child, eight fathered two or three children, and one fathered five children. The respondents fathered a total of thirty-eight children and an average of two. Nevertheless, ten of the men fathered children by only one female, eight fathered children by two women, and one by three women. Hence, almost half of the respondents were fathers twice or more with more than one woman as mother of their children. Nine respondents desired the women to become mothers of their children while four did not. Beside, two respondents wanted a child by the mother of their first two children, but not the second mother; and two desired the second mother who birthed two children, yet they did not want the first women to bear children. When the latter distinction was made, usually the men had become disinterested in the mothers of their children.

Since the respondents were not married to the mothers of their children, we asked them whether they were their favorite girlfriends at the onset of fatherhood. Of the seventeen fathers responding, the mothers were the favorite girlfriends of thirteen; however, four did not consider the women their favorite girl-friends.

Home Sex Education

The sex education that parents of the respondents taught them is a relevant backdrop for understanding single parenthood. According to the respondents, their fathers had warned them about sex and girls. For example, they were told not to touch everything they see; hence, a girl's availability should not be the only criterion for sexual activity. The fathers of the respondents also warned, "There are a lot of diseases out there." One respondent, when he was thirteen, found out from a twenty-one year old woman; for example, he noted, "I was on the swimming team and I taught her to swim. On one occasion, she carried me to a hotel and it was fun; it was a one night stand because she was married." Nevertheless, the respondent says, "I contracted a venereal disease." Also, a father informed one respondent, "Thirty or forty minutes of fun aren't worth taking care of a girl and baby eighteen years." According to this respondent, his daddy was right. Still other fathers advised the respondents, "If you find a nice woman, engage in sex, but don't get her pregnant," "Treat them (women) right. Take care of them, Never neglect them," and, as if to anticipate what could happen, another father suggested, "You should get a job before engaging in sex." Still, another respondent noted, "My uncle told me everything. For example, he told

72

us there are three types of women; one type is fast and sex oriented, another is quiet and gets men married fast, and the third type is called a broad and searches for men in the streets." On the other hand, there were six respondents who related their fathers did not tell them much about girls and sex. For example, according to two respondents, "I learned on my own because he left us at an early age; I guess that's what caused me to become a single parent" and "Daddy did not tell me anything about sex and girls, I guess because he didn't think I was sexually active and I wanted to learn on my own." Although one respondent did not answer this question, the remaining five explained that their fathers deceased relatively early in their lives.

It appears that none of the respondents received solid sex education at home. Nonetheless, though a majority of the fathers evaded the subject, a few fathers gave their sons insight into matters of disease, pregnancy, responsibility and types of women. Also, there were mothers who forewarned the respondents about sex and girls. They advised that, if they desired sex, they should get married, watch for diseases, and make sure the girls were protected. Also, according to one single father, his mother warned him to leave girls alone because they would get him in trouble. She suggested that he find a main girl and get married; yet, he did not need her advice. Similarly, a respondent noted, "Mama explained everything. She described the problems and told us from A-Z." In still other cases, mothers tried to warn their sons, before they became fathers, and told them how to prevent fatherhood; and a mother admonished a respondent, "If you father a baby, you must move out of this house." However, one respondent noted, "My mother informed me about sex and pregnancy two years after I became a father; it was then too late." In general, maternal sex eduation was comprised of cautions and threat. Conversely, mothers of eight respondents did not tell them anything about girls and sex.

Even though the respondents' sex education at home was relatively weak, several fathers and mothers provided basic knowledge that could have prevented parenthood. Hence, we asked the respondents whether they used birth control.

73

Relationships

<u>Interpersonal Relations with the Mothers of Their Children</u>

Birth control. Use of birth control is one type of interpersonal relations between the respondents and the mothers of their children. However, at the outset, it should be noted that an examination of the respondents' birth control practices indicates that relatively weak sex education at home is an organizing principle for young adult life, including sex without contraception. Paradoxically, we also found that in homes where parents had given the respondents a relatively good sex education, contraception still was not used.

In general, however, it appears that lack of a solid sex education -- sex abstinence discussions, ongoing dialogue between parents and children and between boyfriends and girlfriends, and children's conviction not be become single parents -- corresponds to non-contraception usage. For example, similar to sex education, there was relatively poor communication between the respondents and their girlfriends about contraception usage. Hence, according to seven respondents, they chose to use contraception and believed their girlfriends were on the pill. For example, one respondent noted, "My mother told me not to make a girl pregnant and I was trying to do what she said. So before my girlfriend became pregnant, I inquired about the pill and she told me she was taking it. That was a fib; I went into the situation thinking I was protected and wasn't. If I had known she wasn't on the pill, I would not have had sex." Similarly, another respondent replied that he did not use condoms because neither girlfriend wanted to use them, nevertheless, because one went to family planning, he took for granted both were using birth control. Therefore, according to these respondents, their girlfriends' pregnancy was a surprise. Similarly, another single father related, "I thought my girlfriends were using birth control." Although another girlfriend had not gone to family planning, the respondent says, he thought she was using contraception. These findings indicate that the respondents and their girlfriends indeed experienced poor communication; moreover, they suggest that men should not assume women are using birth control because they go to family planning. Another implication is that at least one respondent was fooled by his girlfriend; hence, this seems to signal the

74

need for men to use birth control and no longer depend on women. Also, an implication of these findings is that a majority of women attempted to trap the respondents into getting married. Indeed, if this is the case, none succeeded which should serve as a warning to other females with a similar view. In still a different case, because the respondent had used condoms, if he sometimes missed, he thought the girl would not get pregnant. Since women's ovulation cycle is not always predictable, men should not risk pregnancy by believing a certain time of month is safe. In reality, there does not appear to be a safe period; furthermore, use of condoms, at times, does not make women sterile, during future encounters. Hence, it is apparent that the bottom line is a permanent, implemented, contraception image.

On the other hand, the remainder of the sample consciously chose to chance pregnancy. The usual pattern was that the respondents did not like to use condoms. For example, five noted they had gotten tired of using them and wanted the natural feeling. According to another respondent, "Because I objected to them, my girlfriend did not want me to use condoms. I called the shots; in the case of the second child, it was planned and I wanted it." This situation suggests that the respondent totally dominated the sexual process.

Similarly, another father stated, "We did not use contraception because we were trying to get a baby. I felt like I wanted one; I wanted something to be responsible to and let him know about life. Also, my girlfriend wanted a baby at the time she became pregnant." This couple decided to have a family without benefit of marriage; further analysis indicates the respondents desired a child outside marriage the way others desire dates in singlehood. Also, the respondent wanted something to be responsible to but not for; hence, he could have the obligation but not implement it. In the case of another respondent, he noted, "I thought condoms would take away from the feeling; and my girlfriend never asked me to use them. We had sex nine months before she became pregnant; and we have had sex since the baby, unprotected; yet, my girlfriend has not conceived again." This couple suggests still another facet of single parenthood; young men and women play Russian Roulette with their reproductive systems. Furthermore, they risk pregnancy even when there has been a mishap.

Another respondent took a similar view. He noted that contraception had not been used. "It wasn't necessary," he said, "to use condoms because they only qualify if women ask. The averge man does not put on condoms, unless asked. Though I know they irritate and cut down on feelings, to prevent pregnancy, women must ask men to use condoms." Surely, we agree with the respondent; since the disadvantages of single parenthood are weighted on the side of single mothers, women have the authority, albeit the responsibility, regardless of age, to request and require contraception during intercourse. In still another case, the respondent thought that contraception was a waste of sperms. In this case, he was more interested in using one batch of sperms and one sperm at that, since only one sperm can fertilize an egg, than in preventing single parenthood. As I studied his response, I came to the conclusion that probably the respondent was not aware of the fertilization process. On the other hand, one father had a different experience. Because the IUD had been removed, when the mother of his first child became pregnant, she was not using contraception.

The men in this sample confirm that lack of adequate sex education -- ongoing dialogue about consequences of pregnancy, prevention, and conviction not to become single parents -- is indeed a relevant backdrop for understanding single parenthood. Moreover, our findings suggest that several reasons, including pleasure, explain why some black men in Young Park and Calvert Park become fathers before marriage. Also, when young men were convinced not to have children, they at least desired their girlfriends to prevent pregnancy; hence, poor communication led to pregnancy. Similarly, there was only limited or no concern about consequences of sex and pregnancy. Thus, enjoyment, parenthood, and prevention, though inadequate, are the visions of sex life in the sample.

First Reaction Upon Learning They Were Becoming Fathers the First Time. Another type of reaction occurred between the respondents and their girlfriends at the onset of pregnancy. We found that, just as views of prevention differ, responses to impregnating a female the first time also vary widely. One pattern is shock and disappointment. For example, one respondent related, "I was shocked and upset. I asked her not to be pregnant." Of these four men, one had experienced "the scare before." On that occasion, the respondent noted, "My girlfriend told me she was expecting, but I didn't believe her. Her mother called my house and told me I had to tell my parents. I didn't tell them, but the girl's mother told them. The next day my girlfriend informed me that her mama was going to make her have an abortion. I was relieved because I was seventeen years old and didn't have a high school diploma." However, this time his luck changed and he became a father. It would be a good idea for young men who escape fatherhood, because their girlfriends get an abortion or have a false alarm, to use the experience as a teacher; that is, make certain, thereafter, that either there is no sex or that contraception goes with sex. Similarly, a respondent related, "I was scared, shocked, and didn't know how to tell my parents; nor did I know how to act toward the girl. I decided to cut her loose because I didn't know how her parents would take it. They could have said, you better marry my daughter." The circumstance is that the respondent desired the girl for sex, but not for marriage; and pregnancy ruined the boy-girl relationship. It is interesting, as demonstrated in this case, that often single mothers bear children, out of love for men or to honor their request, yet, both reasons lead to loss of men and their love. Perhaps, however, another respondent offers even more lessons in pregnancy prevention. When he learned that he would become a father, he was scared and felt that he had done something wrong. On the basis of the way his girlfriend approached him about the situation, he became upset. Instead of informing him they were becoming parents, he noted, "She acted as if I was responsible." Also, he noted, "She told three other people before she told me; that made me feel excluded. When she first told me, I stopped seeing her for a month and a half. When I accepted the fact, we weren't getting along." In all probability, this case also illustrates the impact of pregnancy on love relationships. In fact, the respondent now has another girlfriend and maintains a "buddy" relationship with the mother of his child. For example, when he has problems with his girlfriend, whom he nicknamed "Worration," he discusses them with the mother of his child and she consoles and gives him positive advice. Also, the respondent noted that, at the time she began expecting their child, he was also courting another young woman. However, when this girlfriend learned about the onset of fatherhood, the respondent says, she felt neglected and discontinued the relationship; even so, she still allows him sexual privileges.

The respondent also related, "I have feelings for both women and courted them at the same time. However, I see the first one on occasions for sex; because the other girl is in Texas, I rarely see her. When the first mother became pregnant, she asked me to marry her. I asked, How can I marry you when I have a girlfriend to whom I am engaged?" It appears this respondent was adamant when his girlfriend attempted to handle their forthcoming parenthood through marriage. However, she responded, "I'll kill you!" "She tried," says the respondent, "to stick me with a pair of scissors, but I did not marry her. However, I had told her that if she got pregnant, I would." The case seems clear. We cannot trust men with our bodies; hence, the response to such promise should be, if you marry me, providing the man is financially, educationally, and occupationally successful, I may get pregnant for you. This case, as well as the sample, illustrates several other lessons that women can learn about men. In essence, a basic lesson is that some men are concerned only about themselves -- a point I think women overlook in sex. Since men think only of themselves, women must have enough self esteem to think only about themselves. This respondent also noted that he had planned to marry the Texas girl, but he got orders to go to Korea. However, he noted, "After I became accustomed to Korean girls, my infatuation with her ended. When I returned from Korea, the Texas mother asked me to marry her. I told her I would not marry her because I felt she had sex with someone else while I was in Korea." The first implication here is that motherhood does not maintain a man's love nor obtain a marriage license. Another implication is that a double standard is held up; a single father can become involved with another woman, but a single mother should remain virtuous. What we have found in our Norfolk State University, college, single mothers' study is that virtue also fails to maintain a man's love and obtain a marriage license. Therefore, if a young woman desires a man as a husband, her best chance results from singlehood without parenthood.

Another pattern was mixed emotions. Hence, one respondent related that he was confused, but after he got used to the idea of becoming a father (two or three days), he became happy. He added, "Then I had a feeling that I had done something I had never experienced. I thought and desired a boy, but I am satisfied with a girl." Another example is the young man

78

who said, "I was happy and upset because I had to get a job and become dependable."

In still three other cases, the third pattern of reaction to forthcoming fatherhood is that the single fathers responded by saying, I expected it and was not shocked; for example, one father noted, "When I learned about it, I knew I needed a job and got one."

The fourth reaction to forthcoming fatherhood was happiness, joy, and enjoyment. For example, one father responded to his girlfriend thusly: "You are lying to me!" She had told him this before and he thought it was true, but it wasn't. This time her mother verified it and he jumped for joy! Two other single fathers were also happy. One noted, "My first reaction was happiness. It made me feel good to think about being a father." The second father replied, "I smiled and said Yeah? I was happy. Then, I said, Well I guess I will accept the responsibility. It was a good feeling seeing her carry my baby. Seeing her stomach made me feel better about becoming a father." He continued, "Now, marriage is a larger thing because it means that one must accept more responsibility and I am not ready for that. A baby is not as much responsibility; and I am only responsible for the baby." The respondents, in general, clarified yet another pattern; that is, they accept limited responsibility for child support, but rarely does support for mothers of their children become a consideration. Hence, our women are willing to bear children, yet not receive personal financial support, a finding that suggests there are those among us who invest too much in our men for what we receive.

Thus, of the nineteen respondents, eight expressed happiness, enjoyment, and joy while three were neutral, and seven were disappointed about becoming fathers the first time. It is apparent that single fatherhood is complex and multiple patterns describe each of its dimensions.

Family Planning. Another area of interpersonal relations is family planning. Similar to reactions toward the onset of fatherhood, the respondents vary widely in family planning. In spite of all respondents not using contraception, at the time of pregnancy, the respondents and their girlfriends were either at odds about parenthood or the men desired children, but not by the women who birthed them, five respondents excepted.

79

One pattern, in the case of these five fathers, is that they and their girlfriends desired a child. For example, a twenty-one year old respondent noted, "We both asked each other for a baby." Now that we have one on the way, it seems to get harder; there is also the pressure of her mother. She wants to make her clean the whole house. The responsibility is also more than I expected. We have found that single parenthood is harder than singlehood. I don't run around and see other women; I gave all them up to be with this one." The five respondents in this group and their girlfriends requested a baby from each other the way others request sex. Nevertheless, they decided that single parenthood is a difficult experience.

Another pattern is that four single fathers desired their children, but the mothers of their children were not ready for pregnancy. One father in this group told us that he wanted a child because all his brothers had kids and he added, "I (he) wanted one too." In the case of another respondent, the first mother of his children became pregnant the second time they had sex while still twelve years old and the second mother became pregnant the first time they had sex. When the second child was born, the respondent was eighteen and she was seventeen and the child is now nine years old. However, he noted, "The mother of my first child was fourteen, when she had our baby and I was fifteen. Because the children are mine, I wanted them." Also, in a third relationship, the respondent wanted his child, but was not sure the mother of the child had the same feeling.

Similarly, the next pattern is that three single fathers desired not to become fathers, but their girlfriends desired motherhood. One of these respondents replied that parenthood was a mistake. In another relationship, the respondent says, though his girlfriend desired conception, he was scared about the responsibility; with the second, he was also scared, and with the third, he was scared, but he got over it; "yet, I hate to see her receive public assistance," he added. And the third respondent noted, "I wasn't ready for a baby because I had not finished school and had no trade; therefore, I was not prepared for responsibility." These findings indicate that three respondents were concerned about responsibility for their children. Therefore, they suggest that male irresponsibility, as a general description for all single fathers, does not adequately describe reality.

Another pattern is that three fathers desired one child, but no more. For example, one single father indicated that he wanted the first mother to have his child because he had somewhat promised he would marry her if she got pregnant. However, "I did not marry her," the respondent says, "because we had differences before pregnancy." On the other hand, he did not want the second mother to bear a child for him. In still another relationship, a respondent with two children, by the same woman, said, "When the first baby came, we desired a baby, when the second came, it wasn't planned. However, we must care about both." In the third situation, a forty-one year old father who has five children, desired only two. The first child was born to his babysitter and conceived the first time they had sex, and, according to him, he "Definitely did not want fatherhood in that relationship." Hence, these respondents do not desire all the children fathered; on this basis, we concluded that number of children is not necessarily related to desire for number of children fathered. Consequently, the problem of single fatherhood seems to beg a solution.

The final pattern is that neither the single fathers in this sample nor their girlfriends desired parenthood. One of these two fathers noted, "I did not want a baby, however, I felt like I was ready to accept the responsibility." This finding also indicates that, among black single fathers, premarital fatherhood is solution-oriented.

It is apparent that in general family planning among the respondents mainly involved desire for children. Because this was apparent, we sought to determine whether the respondents and their girlfriends had made economic plans for their children.

Boyfriend and girlfriend discussions. We asked the fathers in our study whether they and the mothers of their children had discussed, prior to conception, how the baby would be supported economically. Several patterns were noted, including conversation about child support. A nineteen year old father of a baby boy is the only one who had discussed the matter beforehand; he had told his girlfriend he would support the baby with earnings from his job. Another pattern was post-conception planning. Thus, after the baby was conceived, eleven of the respondents and their girlfriends decided the economic support of their children. One of these fathers provides half the support for his first child and all the support for his second child and both mothers work; therefore, neither child is receiving public assistance. Four working fathers give their children support and would like to support them entirely; another father and his girlfriend work and support their child without welfare assistance; on the other hand, still another respondent decided to get a job, but could not find one. In addition, a twenty-three year old father with two children, one by different mothers, related, "I support one child as much as I can and slip the child's mother a couple of dollars now and then. Concerning the second mother, because she thought we were going to get married, we never discussed it." Then a twenty-two year old father of two children, by the same mother, supports his family and pays half of Medicaid. Beside, a twenty-three year old father of one child stated, "I told my girlfriend I would keep a job and support the baby. It does not matter what kind of job, as long as I provide support because odds and ends are needed"; the father is a cook. Similarly, a twenty-three year old father of three related that during the first pregnancy, he stopped school, got a job, and helped support the mother of his children. These findings indicate that several of the respondents do not rely on the welfare system to support their children -- another indication of emerging responsible parenthood among the respondents and the mothers of their children.

A final pattern is vague concerning children's economic welfare. For example, a father noted, "We did not discuss anything about a baby. I didn't think about her getting pregnant because she said, 'Don't worry.' I figured she couldn't get pregnant. However, one day, she said, 'Sammy, I am pregnant,' I replied, I thought you said don't worry! She said, 'I made a mistake.' My answer was, you sure did! Because she figured I wasn't going to support the baby, she was three months pregnant before she let me know. We only had sex occasionally. You could say I was messing around with her; my main girl was on the pill." He continued, "Although I had a main girl, I went out and got somebody else; I wish I hadn't found her." This respondent is another one who does not desire fatherhood, at least, with this mother. He continued, "I am still having sex with the mother of my child, however, beforehand, I make sure she swallows the pill, because I recently put in a new diehard battery, meaning set of sperms. Also, she pays me $20.00 each time we have sex." Because the mother of his child had disappointed him, child support was not uppermost in his mind; and she pays him for sex support. Certainly, the mother of his child affords several observations; one is that she appears to have a low self image. That is, if she cannot defer sex, it appears that she would not obtain sexual favors by paying the father of her child. It is also apparent that the respondents and their girlfriends became parents without discussing how the children would be supported.

Ways the respondents show the mothers of their children love. Since the men are not very economically responsive to the mothers of their children, we next determined the love support they give them. We began by asking: After your girlfriend told you that she was expecting your child, did you love her more or less? Concerning the only mother of a man's children, of the ten respondents with one child, three noted they loved their girlfriend the same while seven said they loved her more. The reasons the men gave for loving their girlfriends more were: "I knew I had to take care of her," "She was carrying something that was a part of me," "She was bringing something into the world I really wanted," and "I knew the baby would bring us closer together and we would be a family." Also, according to these respondents, they loved their girlfriends more because they were becoming mothers of their children and one noted, "Because I had a problem, when we met, I needed someone to be with. Because I always mingled with girls, my friends called me a freak (sexually permissive). About six years ago, my girlfriend was willing to chance me and give me a child."

Then, one respondent indicated that he loved his girlfriend less because "She did not tell him about his forthcoming fatherhood from day one." Another noted, "It upset me because she had done something to me by not protecting herself. I figured that's why she didn't tell me."

Turning to five of the respondents, with more than one mother of their children, we find that one loves all four of the women, who birthed a child for him, the same as before they became pregnant, while a father of two children, by different mothers, loved the first mother less because he was scared. He also noted, "I did not want to get married, but I loved the second mother more because we both wanted a baby." In a similar

83

situation, we found that a respondent still had emotional feelings for the first mother, but he could not get back into the relationship because he is not satisfied with what she does (unfaithfulness); however, the second woman is his fiancee and they have faith in each other. Another respondent with the same number of children and girlfriends loved them more because he wanted a baby and marriage while the father of five children related that he loved both women involved more because it gave him a good feeling for them to carry his children.

Next, we studied the sexual feelings of the respondents after they received the news of forthcoming fatherhood. There are various patterns. For example, one pattern is inaccessibility; an incarcerated respondent did not have access to his girlfriend while she was pregnant. On the other hand, another pattern was fluctuation; hence, romantic feelings decreased while at other times they increased. The third pattern was decrease in sexual interest; and the fourth pattern, according to six respondents, was that romantic interests remained unchanged. Similarly, the fifth pattern, as noted by six other respondents, was that respondents' sexual interest in the mothers of their children increased during pregnancy because they had no other choice, had to abstain from sex for a while, which heightened desire, and their girlfriends were more appealing. In the latter instance, the man lost his girlfriend to another man, and according to him, he did not know what he had until he lost her.

Current relationships with the mothers of their children. To get a better handle on the emotional relationship between the respondents and the mothers of their children, we asked the respondents to describe their current relationships to the mothers of their first child. Of the ten respondents answering this question, their responses are noted below. One pattern is that four couples get along; hence, they related:

> We get along well, engage in activities, and spend time together.

> Up to this point, I am happy. If we did not have sex, it would still be perfect; we teach each other things.

> I can talk with the first one because she is older.

She wakes and kisses me and the baby is three months old.

We are friends. I want us to get back together. I can't take her back now because I am living with someone else.

The second pattern is that relations are fraught with difficulties, as shown in the respondents' description:

We get along well. We only argue and shove each other back and forth. Because we know each other's needs, we get along together.

We have a cut and dry argument and we argue about everything, but we do not fight. We broke up. I left because I was bored and tired. Also, she wanted me to be henpecked and I did not want to act henpecked. Beside, I could not have any friends. Regarding the second mother, she left me because she said that I was sexually more than she could handle; now I have three girlfriends.

It is a cutthroat relationship that has ended. I broke her heart and pride, kicked her, and enjoyed other women.

Both of us were in love, but not anymore.

The first mother married another man while the second and third mothers are with someone else.

Economic difficulties are keeping us down. If we had money, we could be a lot happier (my girlfriend is a senior at Norfolk State University). We don't want to get married until we can take care of everything. I worry about our children's name. Their mother decided that, when we get married, we will change their last name. When I feel that we are strong enough to take care of each other, financially, we will marry. I like to make my own money. If she works, it is her life, but I don't want her to take care of me. (Hence, one respondent is not willing to marry a woman to benefit from her achievement; in fact, when they get married, he wants to be equal to her in earnings.)

85

Why Not Marriage? After finding that the men desired father-hood, yet only one planned to marry the mother of his child, it seemed important to ask why they did not marry the first girl who mothered their child. The men gave several reasons for not marrying the women; for example, they noted that marriage was too much responsibility. One of these respondents replied that when his salary is better, he will marry the mother of his child. Another respondent, who loves the first mother of his children now more than before, would have married her, if he could have afforded it. While talking, he pointed to an attractive petite girl and said, "There she is on the porch. I love her because she has stuck with me as I went in and out of reform schools and the penitentiary."

Another theme the respondents used to explain why they had not married the first mother of their children is they were not ready. They noted, for example: "I wasn't ready because I like fun," or "I wasn't ready mentally nor financially." Also, one respondent enjoys fatherhood, but he does not want marriage because it would deprive him of the freedom to come and go as he pleases. Similarly, another respondent is not ready for marriage, he says, because he has a little devil in him that still likes to play and he does not get enough satisfaction from the mother of his child. Also, he has found his girlfriend, whom he nicknamed "Worration," more trouble than the mother of his child; and he is not ready to give up dancing and the streets.

Beside responsibility and deprivation of freedom, the respondents gave a number of other reasons for not marrying the first mother of their children. It did not occur, they say, because the women were unfaithful, they did not love them enough for marriage, preferred the girl who did not become a mother, and a grandmother, incarceration, and financial instability prevented it.

Also, the men used other reasons for not marrying the first mother of their children. For example, the respondents did not want all their children; and some men created discord in their relationships with the mothers of their children, which precluded marriage.

Nevertheless, it is apparent that some respondents' girlfriends attempted to find ways to hold them. For example, unbeknowing to their boyfriends, they did not practice birth control; moreover, at least one girl, against the wishes of her boyfriend, gave their children her last name instead of his name. And explained that, after marriage she would give the children his name. It is likely that his girlfriend is using his intense desire for his children to carry his last name as a last resort to obtain a marriage license.

Relationship Between the Respondents and Their Children

Child support. After determining that the economic support of children was not usually a pre-pregnancy consideration, we asked the respondents to describe child support. We found that the support system includes three identifiable patterns. One is that four respondents give their children a specified amount of support at specified times. For example, one father provides all the financial support for his two children, by two mothers, along with the women's help, except one half of Medicaid, and buys them everything they need while another gives each of two mothers of his two children $50-$100 a week. A third father gives the mother of his first child $40 a week, but he does not give the second mother of his second child any support because she is financially stable. On the other hand, a father of one boy contributes $100 a week in child support.

The second pattern of economic support is vague and the men described it in such terms as, "I give the first mother money for the children, but not the other two mothers," "If she calls and says she needs something, I take it to her and we go shopping together," "I give her money for the child every week and buy things when the baby needs them," "I take care of the first three children, but not the fourth," and "I do not give the mother money, but when I take them shopping, I spend $100 on the mother and child."

On the other hand, the third pattern of child support is benign neglect. According to eight of the respondents, they do not support their children.

The way the respondents show their children love. The next determinant of the nature of the fathers' interaction with their children is the love they demonstrate to their children. Similar to economic support, one pattern is benign neglect while another is demonstration of love. For example, the respondents show their children love by visiting, caring, giving, hugging, kissing and squeezing them. Also, they show it by going on walks, taking the children to the movies, baby sitting, daily visiting, or taking them to their homes. Beside, because their mothers do not want them, a forty-one year old respondent, with the help of his mother and his oldest son, are raising his other three children. Also, another respondent loves his four year old son; and takes him to his house on weekends. This father also baby sits while the mother goes out; in reality, he says, "My family and I baby sit and my second child, by another mother, is one year old and we talk on the telephone."

One of the interesting patterns about economic and emotional support is that only three fathers do not show their children love, but fewer fathers give their children economic support. Moreover, another finding is that the men are often vague about their economic support, however, they are very clear about the love they show their children. Still another point is that though economic support is weaker than emotional support, in almost all cases, emotional and economic support are ephemeral, at its best. What this means is that the respondents' children are deprived of solid economic and emotional support from their fathers, just as the latter were deprived of solid sex education at home. Moreover, among the men who support their children, usually there is no attempt to support the mothers of their children.

The meaning of fatherhood. Because in general the respondents experience a weak emotional bond with the mothers of their children, because child support is inadequate, we next determined the meaning of fatherhood. We found that fatherhood means different things to the respondents. Six talked about life as a single father. For example, one father related that he and his girlfriend thought it would be difficult the first few months, but fun and exciting to see the baby grow. Another father related that it entails staying up with the baby, paying bills, and deciding who will keep the baby (the fathers baby sit and take the children to their homes). Also, one father said that he likes to go out and meet people and is not the fatherly type. Another noted, "We knew we could not go out like we use to; at first, it bothered us, but as we got older, it was okay." On the other hand, a respondent noted, "While

I was in prison, I thought about it, but things changed after I got out. That is, my girlfriend became pregnant by another man." Additionally, a respondent related, "I thought it would be different taking care of someone. It is very hard and a new experience."

We also asked the respondents to identify the various meanings of fatherhood. For some, it means an improved self image. An example is a respondent who noted that "Fatherhood means I feel good knowing there is someone in the world who is part of me." Similarly, a respondent related, "It makes me feel proud when my chidren call me Daddy. Most fathers are gone and the children only have their mothers. My father left, but I don't plan to leave my children because I know how hard it was for my mother to take care of six kids. I plan to be with my children until the day I die." Not unlike these responses, another respondent related, "Fatherhood makes me feel good, gives me a sense of responsibility, and the opportunity to show children the right way to go."

The responsibility theme was strong in the father's responses. Hence, one father lamented that he couldn't support the mother and his child while another said, "Caring for a baby is hard." Of course, some of the respondents spoke about responsibility in a more optimistic fashion. Therefore, they noted that fatherhood makes them feel alright and responsible, assume the role of leadership, spend time with their children, and enjoy their company. Also, one respondent, on this same theme, noted, "It shows me that I can't run the streets because I have to support my daughter." And a father of four children, by different mothers, related that fatherhood "Makes me feel like I am 110 percent man." Though not solid, the meaning of fatherhood indicates as emerging sense of responsibility for the welfare of their children as well as a source of their self-image.

Relationship With Their Mothers

The reaction of the respondent's mothers to news of their sons' forthcoming fatherhood. We were mainly interested in the interaction between the respondents and their mothers when they told them they were becoming fathers the first time. Because some research has described single mothers and their families, we asked the single fathers to describe the reactions of their mothers when they learned they would soon become fathers. Again, there was no single pattern; for example, we found that some mothers did not know or did not respond. Beside, there were mothers who seemed resigned to the notion of sons who were also single fathers, as indicated in the individual responses from varied mothers. For example, one respondent noted, "My mother wasn't surprised. Because the rest of her children, my three brothers, were single parents, she said that it was about time for me to become a father." Similarly, a respondent's mother said, "I knew it was about time. However, you don't look like the fatherly type, therefore, I did not think you would become a father." In another case, a respondent noted, "My girlfriend told my mother she was going to have her son's child. Then, my mother told me about it. And said it was about time, because she thought I was quiet."

But there is more to the responses of the respondents' mothers. In fact, some of the women demonstrated attitudes of sarcasm and anger. For example, according to one respondent, "My mother told me, welcome to the world; and to do better by my child than she did by me (she held grudges against me)" while another respondent's mother replied, "Now its time to be a man. There is no time for playing. It takes money to bring a child into the world"; and another respondent's mother told him, "Congratulations! But don't bring them (mother and child) home. You better take care of it because I am not going to take care of your child." She also asked him whether he planned marriage; his answer was "No." Also a respondent noted, "The first time I became a father, mother was upset. She said, 'You are going to take full responsibility for it; and I am going to make sure of it.' I saw a speck of guilt because she never sat down and talked to me about such matters."

In Retrospect

Since marriage and children were perceived as responsibility and curtailment of freedom, some children were desired while others were not, we asked the respondents whether they had any regrets about single fatherhood. A related question was whether, if they could start life over, would they live it differently. And, if so how?

Out of the nineteen single fathers, only two noted they would live their lives the same way. One of them answered, "I have no regrets about being a single father. If I could start over and know what I know now, I probably would live the same way. My life is exciting and enjoyable." Similarly, the second single father noted, "I am happy and satisfied with my life."

Even so, the remainder of the sample gave several ways they would change their lives. For example, one noted that instead of incarceration, he would be "pushing" an eight hour day. Another way the respondents would change their lives includes becoming fathers of children only by one woman. Also, they would use condoms, make sure their girlfriends use contraception, further their education, give children their last name and become better off financially. Additional information from the fathers also vivifies how the respondents would live their lives differently, if they had a second chance. One respondent replied, "Life would be a whole lot different. I would be a virgin. I wouldn't jump right into it. I would ask her a thousand questions dealing with the pill. The unfortunte thing is that when the child goes to school, children are going to ask, where is your Dad? He's going to have a hard time explaining he doesn't know." Another respondent said he would change everything. He would wait to engage in sex, finish high school, and think about going to college. He regrets fatherhood because it alters one's plans. Several of the other respondents noted they would use condoms, even if the girls said no, and get married before having children. Another respondent, according to him, would use discretion and would not have a baby at nineteen because he was too immature; instead, he would get married at twenty-five. The remainder of the respondents indicated they would use condoms and some fathers stated they would also require their girlfriends to use contraceptives. Further, they noted they would try not to impregnate a girl and get married, if they desired children.

Discussion

This discussion abstracts two principal elements from the lives of the respondents in this study. The first concerns the principal findings while the second is about single fatherhood prevention. In the latter discussion, first, the preventions the respondents indicated would have prevented them from becoming single fathers are described and, next, the preventions shown in the findings are noted.

Female Roles in the Respondents' Sex Life

To begin, we shall discuss the main findings. They include female roles in the sex life of the respondents, preventive sex education, violation of birth control norms, and results.

Careful study of the findings indicates that females have made an enormous contribution to the development of the respondents' sex life. Even from the beginning, three female baby sitters, one girlfriend -- without request from respondent, and four girlfriends, in agreement with four respondents, initiated their first sex experience. In terms of numbers, eight of the nineteen fathers began their sex life because females introduced them or jointly made the decision with them. Moreover, seven girlfriends of seven different respondents led them to believe they were using birth control; one female told a respondent that she was using contraception. Beside, in general, the girlfriends of the respondents were not favorable toward male contraception and, when they were, they still placed their bodies at the discretion of the respondents. A related point is that a few girlfriends desired babies when the respondents did not want to become fathers. Apparently, because it was ego-satisfying, the men complied; nevertheless, in such cases, single parenthood was initiated by females. Once the women became single parents, many of them continued to chance pregnancy, which resulted in expandng a few men's fatherhood.

Because the respondents usually desired children, it appears that the women considered themselves fortunate to be able to do something for their boyfriends they could not do for themselves. Once they had obliged the men, the women discovered a life that robbed them of the men's love for whom they implemented an act that only women can achieve. It is at this stage the women learned that, instead of an enjoyable relationship, in general, they experienced verbal, physical, and emotional abuse and became enemies, friends, buddies, or partners in caring for their children, while other women became their girlfriends. There were many more discoveries the mothers of the respondents' children made. They learned that the men considered them a nuisance, did not love them enough to get married, and babies do not necessarily guarantee marriage licenses. Also, they learned that the men for whom they had children did not always want them to become mothers of their children; surely, this hints at a degree of pride, concern about individuals who would be called the mothers of their children. This is indeed a significant lesson for women to learn; if they use norms of the society for selecting prospective parents, surely they will either find a different type of man to father their children or refrain from bearing children. And the climax to the entire situation is that the men, two excepted, wish they were not single fathers; therefore, an act of motherhood that changed their girlfriends' lives as well as their own, is one the respondents wish had never happened.

Preventive Sex Education, Violation of Norms and Results

Though eight respondents had not received sex education at home, close analysis of home, sex training suggests that it was not enough to be preventive. Yet, not only were eight respondents not privileged to sex education, but also the remainder of the sample violated birth control norms. It is a truism that the respondents and their girlfriends blatantly violated the norms. One must ask, Why? We can only surmise that several reasons explain the trend; one is that women did not fear pregnancy because they believed it was the route either to a marriage license or a long-term relationship with their boyfriends. Some related evidence of this observation is the practice of one female's refusal, prior to anticipated marriage, to give her three children the last name of her boyfriend. Further, in our opinion, blatant violation of birth control norms resulted from a somewhat weak character structure. By character, we mean moral strength. It thus appears that a sex education program should include black male sex power -- sexual abstinence, or infrequent sex with unswerving use of contraception, sex participation only with girls who have sex and blood power, and absolute refusal to become single fathers. What are the results of violation of birth control norms? As shown in the respondents data, family disruption is one result. With the birth of children, mothers were hurt and their sons' lives were adversely altered; moreover, the mothers of their children were placed at a disadvantage. Hence, there is not much in single parenthood for either the mother or the father.

What's in Single Fatherhood for Men?

Starting with the father, we asked of the data, specifically, What's in single parenthood for black men? We found they are the beneficiaries of unpleasant relationships with the mothers of their children, a weakened emotional bond between themselves and the mothers of their children, financial responsibility unequal to their assets, disruption of achievement goals, unhappy mothers, and disfigurement of female bodies. Moreover, the respondents received the title of daddy, which resulted in what we respectfully call here -- Toddler manhood -- fathers with inadequate emotional, occupational and economic resources. And they use their children as marks of achievement -- a feat that any normal menstruating girl and thirteen year old boy can achieve. What is needed is more character, courage, and disciplining where it counts, family and self respect, black male sex and sperm control power, good citizenship, education, and employment. The respondents' data also hint at what's in single parenthood for the mothers of their children. They seem to suggest that women deprive themselves, socially, emotionally, academically, and financially. Also, as mentioned earlier, mothers of the respondents' children learned that babies do not make marriages and, like the fathers of their children, it dwarfs their status; they must assume the major responsibility for their children and often do not escape the burdensome task of difficult survival.

Though, we recognize dwarfed parenthood in the respondents, there is an emerging pattern of male responsibility. For example, it is seen in those respondents who desired their girlfriends to use contraception and in the one respondent who now watches his girlfriend swallow the pill, before sex. Also, it is seen in a few of the men who were not ready to become fathers because of their financial situation; and in the fathers who contribute minimal support as well as those who provide specified amounts at specified times for their children, and in the love support they show them. Thus, it seems that ephemeral male responsibility, and a majority of the respondents make some type of contribution to their children, is a good start for stemming the tide of single parenthood. Another possible intervention strategy is sound training in male human sexuality -- responsible sex, sex power, sperm control power, responsibility for one's children, personal pride, love and respect for all black women, communication about contraception, an implemented contraception image, strong interpersonal relations with people who seek to achieve, character, good citizenship, courage, and the incentive to use one's abilities to become "self actualizing" - realize one's fullest potential, which is not single parenthood.

Fatherhood Prevention: Ways the Respondents' Fatherhood Could Have Been Circumvented

The second phase, as noted earlier, concerns fatherhood prevention. First, we will report what the respondents noted, in direct response to our inquiry, What could have been done or said that would hve prevented them from becoming single fathers?

In response to the question of prevention, we received varied responses. For example, because of their compelling desire for sex or children, a few respondents noted that nothing could have been done; that is, as one respondent replied, "I was in heat and had lost control, however, my girlfriend wasn't in heat." On the other hand, some of the respondents indicated they could have been responsible enough to use protection. Still other respondents noted their fatherhood could have been prevented by watching their girlfriends take the pill and using condoms. Also, their fatherhood could have been prevented, they say, if the girls had been more sexually responsible. According to one respondent, "Since the girl doesn't want to get pregnant, if she cared about herself, she would use contraception." In this connection, one respondent noted that, "Girls should be taught to use protection because they are just as much at fault, when pregnancy occurs as men. If they would push the issue, he continued, we would use them because we will only go as far as women let us. This is true because we don't want to go to jail for rape." Similarly, a respondent said, "The girl should say no, I cannot have sex. Mom and Dad would not approve." "The girl," he says, "has to bear the pressure while a guy can do what he wants." The emphasis on the need for girls to protect their bodies is supported by the casual way a nineteen year old father, in our sample, views women. He said, that he likes his race car better than women. Further, he noted, "After I get what I want from a woman, she can go. I don't touch the mother of my child too often. I don't trust women any further than I can see them. A woman will be in your face now and an hour later she will find another man. If she takes my money and gives it to another, I would kill both." He keeps his son because he gets tired of hearing the child's mother ask for money; also, he related, "I get tired of being with the same woman; I want to see a large number of women and don't need a main woman. I work every day, therefore, I don't need her to give me anything. What I need, such as a new race car, she cannot afford," he continued. Careful attention to what the respondent has noted, suggests there are men who desire women only for sex, believe women are weak sexually, to the point, they can see two men in a short span of time, and they are intolerant of requests for child support from the mothers of their children. Furthermore, he suggests that, rather than one woman, he likes variety in women. As a result, it behooves young women to study young men and vice versa because they are preparing for a test -- courtship and sex -- that could determine the rest of their life. What I am attempting to pinpoint is that black women should fully understand our men and act responsibly; if they are quiet and refuse to display themselves, it is worth considering changing men. As the data in this chapter suggest, one cannot get to know a man by only what he says; hence, it takes time and varied difficult circumstances for black females to make informed decisions about sex with our men. Hence, if we are to stem the tide of single parenthood, as much as we desire, it is also important to defer sex in friendship at least a year; without such restraint, we place our lives in potentially serious jeopardy. The question therefore is whether we prefer deferred sexual gratification -- sex power -- or early sexual gratification with adverse, single, parenthood experiences.

Turning next to the solutions abstracted from the findings, the respondents provide additional solutions to single parenthood. The sexuality of the respondents researched for this chapter involves sex education, use of birth control, desire for children, reactions of mothers, family planning, communication with girlfriends, economic and emotional support for their children, and women who birthed them, the meaning of fatherhood, reasons for not getting married, and what they would do, if they could start life over. In general, the sexuality of the respondents is not adequately developed. Starting with their birth status, six of the nineteen men were born to single parents; hence, almost one third of the sample did not have the benefit of a two parent home. As a result, the home personnel structure for human sexuality training was incomplete. A related factor is that eighteen respondents engaged in sex the first time between five and seventeen years of age and eleven fathered their first child between fifteen and nineteen years of age; moreover, eight fathered children by more than one female. Beside, four of the men became fathers in relationships with females who were not their favorite girlfriends. Hence, early sex and fatherhood, fatherhood two or more times, two or more mothers of children, and weak emotional relations with the mothers of one's children indicate the need for a home sex education program. Also, as noted by the respondents and their mothers, younger brothers who become single fathers are sometimes siblings of older brothers who are already single fathers. Hence, our study indicates intragenerational perpetuation of single fatherhood. If it continues to increase, single fatherhood may reach unusual proportions.

Failure to use birth control is another indication of weakly developed human sexuality. Thus, we found that the respondents also experienced poor communication with their girlfriends regarding their use of contraception; moreover, they nor their girlfriends desired babies, yet there was no family planning. In general when the respondents learned about the onset of fatherhood, only seven were happy; hence, except for two fathers, fatherhood did not enrich their self image and, when it occurred, it was merely surface satisfaction. Thus, seventeen noted that, if they could start life over with their present experience, they would not risk fatherhood. Therefore, the very act of becoming a parent, one element in one's sexuality, was a premature and unsatisfying experience; moreover, the response from some of their mothers also indicates that interpersonal relations with their mothers, a significant part of their human sexuality, was strained and therefore weakly developed. And, the relationship between themselves and the mothers of their children was too weak to result in marriage.

We, thus, concluded that the human sexuality -- interpersonal relations with girlfriends and parents, self image, respect for black womanhood, and sex management -- of our men needs improvement through a strong home sex education program. We recommend that men in church, civic, social and Greek Letter organizations help parents assume this responsibility. On the basis of our findings, we recommend the model in Chapter Eight.

The Principle of Legitimacy Exists in Norfolk, Virginia

As seen in retrospect, except two fathers, Malinowski's Principle of Legitimacy is significant. It is apparent that after becoming fathers, the respondents realized the importance of adhering to Malinowski's sociological law; an observation that seems supported by the men's reactions to becoming fathers. Perhaps one way to promote adherence is implementation of pre-pregnancy fatherhood programs that verify the stark reality of single fatherhood.

The Culture of Poverty

The next task is to test Oscar Lewis' Culture of Poverty model (1965) in our findings. Starting with the subculture level, the Norfolk male respondents demonstrate some of its characteristics. One trait is deprivation (Lewis 1965). It is seen in their poor education, as also found by Clark (1965), Rutledge and Gass (1968), Schulz (1969), Rainwater (1971), and Harrington (1972), because it ranges from the seventh grade to more than three years of college. Similarly, the respondents support the view that the poor experience unemployment, underemployment, low wages, and a chronic shortage of cash, as also noted by Clark (1965); Moynihan (1967); Liebow (1967); Hannerz (1969); Ryan (1971); and Rainwater (1971).

Furthermore, the findings in our Norfolk study support a number of family traits, in the poverty subculture, including "the absence of childhood as a specially prolonged and protected stages in the life cycle (and) early initiation into sex" (Lewis 1965). Hence, eighteen of the nineteen respondents first experienced sex between age five and seventeen; and eleven fathered their first child between age fifteen and nineteen. Moreover, they support Lewis' view of "a strong disposition to authoritarianism" (1965), as noted in their decision not to use condoms. Moreover, the findings support the trait of abandonment of wives (girl-friends in the Norfolk study) and children (Lewis 1965). Though a majority of the men want children, the women are abandoned economically and emotionally. Also, the findings partially support the trait of verbal emphasis upon family solidarity (Lewis 1965). The men speak about solidarity with children; however, the dominant pattern with the mothers of their children is low emotional support, along with less then adequate support for their children. The respondents are preoccupied with fun, enjoyment, and making babies for self enhancement rather than concern for women. The men appear to be too involved with themselves to get into the lives of women and make a positive difference. Furthermore, because almost all their children live with their girlfriends, the respondents support the trait of female or mother centered families (Lewis 1965).

Expansion of the Culture of Poverty Model

Beside supporting the culture of poverty, the findings about single fathers in Young and Calvert Parks indicate that it would be useful to expand the model on the subculture level. One recommendation is that the welfare system's relatively slow procedure for obtaining child support from fathers hinders females, because they cannot affort to wait for financial help, from telling the department the location of the fathers of their children. Alone, this factor, thoroughly understood by young unmarried black men, enhances single parenthood because they need not fear concrete responsibility for children whom they father. With a modification of the welfare procedure, we can obtain a better perspective of whether black men who fail to support their children are irresponsible or merely feel that the system owes them something -- support of their children -- or they desire children because they know economic responsibility is tied to government support.

Our findings also suggest other additions to the culture of poverty on the family level. One trait is that females, including baby sitters and girlfriends, often initiate boys into sex life at an early age; moreover, usually they dislike condoms, which often leads to pregnancy; and request babies from their boyfriends, even when the men do not desire fatherhood. Another family trait is that after conception and childbirth, instead of an enjoyable relationship with the fathers of their children, usually they become enemies, friends, buddies, or partners in caring for their child while other women become the men's girlfriends; moreover, the respondents' girlfriends experience girlfriend abuse, including physical, economic, emotional, and verbal behavior. These findings seem to suggest that men, though they tell women differently, do not love women who deprive themselves for their satisfaction.

Modification of the Culture of Poverty Model

Subcultural/Larger Society Model

On the subculture level, instead of unemployment, as indicated by the poverty model, thirteen respondents were employed. Moreover, though there is a chronic shortage of cash among respondents, at least two of the nineteen respondents receive wages that in time are likely to make them adequate providers for their families.

Family Level

Furthermore, on the family level, in the culture of the poor, there is ephemeral sex education and an emerging pattern of male responsibility for children as shown in limited economic help as well as recognition of their economic responsibility for their children along with relatively strong parent-child emotional bonds. Another modification is that instead of several children, ten respondents were fathers only once. A related modification concerns self-perpetuating poverty; instead of perpetuating single parenthood, our findings indicate that twelve (two-thirds) of eighteen respondents were born to married parents. Varied other findings indicate variance from the culture of poverty model. They include the findings that three respondents were neutral and seven were disappointed about their girlfriends' pregnancies; and sixteen respondents express ephemeral love to their children.

Individual Level

We also recommend modification of the model on the individual level of poverty. Oscar Lewis noted that "On the level of the individual the major characteristics are a strong feeling of marginality, of helplessnes, and dependence and of inferiority (1965:xlvii). Our recommendation for Lewis' individual level of poverty describes the deep feelings about fatherhood which contradict surface appearances. Hence, deeper probing revealed that though the men love their children, if they could live their lives over and know what they have experienced, seventeen of the nineteen respondents would put women aside until they complete their education or use condoms and see that their girlfriends use contraception, dedicate themselves to one woman at a time, and if they, by accident, became fathers, before marriage, they would give the children their names. The modification is that the surface appearance of happiness derived from single parenthood does not express the deep feelings about the men's preferred status. Because of this finding, we modify the model to indicate that the respondents' preferred status is singlehood without parenthood. Several other findings indicate modification of the Culture of Poverty model. They include seven respondents' desire for their girlfriends to use birth control and four men did not want particular women to become mothers of their children -- an indication of somewhat positive self image.

Further, similar to females in the preceding chapters, we recommend these modifications to the culture of poverty because of variation in all patterns of fatherhood life. If there is variation among nineteen men, in the same urban, poverty setting, it is likely that variation occurs in all traits of the culture of poverty on the subculture and family level as well as additional traits, including the ones identified in this analysis.

Hence, we believe that the additional findings in this study, suggested for inclusion as traits in the Culture of Poverty model on the subculture, family, and individual level, and modification of the Culture of Poverty Model on the subcultural, family, and individual level will prove useful in understanding and eliminating the worldwide culture of the poor, especially among urban, poor, black, single, fathers and mothers.

CHAPTER SIX

SUMMARY

Introduction

This work is based on five studies of black single parenthood, a 1971 study comprised of forty-six single mothers, a 1978 study with forty-four single mothers, a 1981 sub-study comprised of twenty-three teens expecting their first baby, a 1986 study of twenty-nine single mothers, and a 1986 study comprised of nineteen single fathers in Norfolk, Virginia. However, the 1978 study also includes single mothers in the cities of Norfolk, Virginia Beach, Portsmouth, Chesapeake, Suffolk, and Hampton. This longitudinal analysis of single parenthood resulted from our interest in studying the subject intensively to determine the economic, social, and emotional reality of single parenthood and its solutions along with single parents' views in retrospect. This chapter seeks to summarize the findings in the five studies, note that the Norfolk and Tidewater, Virginia respondents support Malinowski's Principle of Legitimacy, indicate that the 1986 male and female respondents indicate support for Oscar Lewis' Culture of Poverty model, demonstrate that the 1986 findings modify Lewis' Culture of Poverty model, illustrate that the 1986 studies also provide a Self-Correcting Poverty proposition, note that the five studies suggest the solvability of single parenthood, and relate data-based hypotheses, based on the five studies, for further single, black, parenthood research.

We began the five studies with Karma's history as a single mother. As we have seen, Karma's life set the tone for what we described first in each study and later in the entire book. Though the individual studies, in this work, provide expanded knowledge of single parenthood, there are patterns in Karma's (a respondent in the 1986 single mothers' study) life replicated in the lives of the remaining 160 respondents. For example, there are multiple sources of economic and emotional support,

102

agony, absence of father, loneliness, and criticism, rejection, and threats in the home, and reliance on family to help manage single parenthood.

Karma's story also provides a comprehensive view of the cycle of sex education at home, pregnancy, childbirth and childrearing. Hence, it provides varied insights into the origin, nature, and solutions to single parenthood. Let us begin with the origin of single parenthood. Karma became a single mother because she desired to rebel against her mother's desire for her to enjoy youth and obtain a good education, love for her boyfriend, failure to use contraception, residence away from home, and possessive love. The intensity of love for a man that Karma can feel is shown in the possessive attitude she has toward her boyfriend, who is not the father of her children. Though she does not have a consuming love for him, she noted that she is unwilling to share him with another woman. An overly possessive woman creates a situation conducive to female abuse; because a woman is highly involved in a man and underinvolved in herself, a man too becomes overly involved in himself at the expense of a female. Our recommendation for single parents' cross-sex relations and single parenthood avoidance is high self-involvement and under male-involvement.

Karma's experience, as a single mother is vivid, including joy. Hence, at first Karma perceived her children, especially the first baby, as a toy. Once the children were no longer infants and toddlers, she says, "the price tag went up" -- motherhood became more difficult. another result is that Karma's children are difficult to rear, which leads to child abuse; for example, confinement to closets for short periods of time. Hence, the father of Karma's children abuses her emotionally and economically and she abuses their children physically and emotionally.

Another result is that Karma must depend on multiple sources of income for survival. They are employment, boyfriend assistance, and public assistance. However, Karma demonstrates that she works and desires to support her children entirely. This attitude derives from personal self respect and the welfare department. Another difficulty of single parenthood is rejection. Though she has a boyfriend, who provide economic and moral support, she is still devoid of the man's love for whom she mothered children; in all probability, although she says that she does not love him, she is hurt because she loved him enough to disobey her mother and yield to his desires; he reciprocated by marrying another woman. Karma was also rejected by her mother, though she, too, is a single parent. Karma's mother demonstrates that not all single parents are favorable toward their daughters perpetuating single motherhood. Another source of rejection is the family of the father of her children. At one time, they treated Karma like a family member, but now they don't communicate. Furthermore, another result of single parenthood is that Karma's children are deprived of the economic and emotional support of their father and request a father the same way other children request shoes, but as Karma says, she cannot buy one in the store. Moreover, another apparent result is that Karma does not have endless love for her children, sometimes perceived to exist; hence, motherhood is not always equivalent to love for one's children nor does it indicate that mothers have no regrets about single parenthood. In fact, Karma says that, if she could start anew with what she knows, she would not become a single mother; instead, she would get an education.

Karma's portrayal of life as a single mother offers a number of solutions. They pertain to individual, family, contraception, and welfare department enhancement. Beginning with individual enhancement, Karma's motive to get even with her mother as well as show her boyfriend love indicates the need for higher self-esteem. A young girl who has high self esteem will not rebel excessively against suggestions for her own self worth. Moreover, intense love for her boyfriend indicates that one solution is to develop the conviction that one must first love herself; personal and family help make this achievement possible. The family solutions include helping young girls develop the conviction they will not participate in social behavior that demeans their self-image. Karma asks that young girls not rebel against their family members; moreover, she says they should not listen to outsiders, instead, they should pay attention to what their parents say. She pleaded to young girls to stop, look, and listen to what their parents are saying. Perhaps Karma is right because sometimes outsiders are underprepared to offer advice in another's best interest. Karma indicates that another solution to single parenthood is birth control. In the final paragraph of her narrative, she pleads to young girls to use every possible means of preventing motherhood;

she also pleads to them to establish achievement goals and pursue them without being distracted. Hence, Karma advises them to depend not upon friends and lovers, but upon themselves. According to Karma's life history, as a single mother, the third solution is enhancement of the welfare department. As the following findings indicate, Karma's experiences set the tone as well as add to the findings of the remaining 160 respondents in this work.

The Five Studies - Background of Study Populations

Sex Involvement

Starting with sex involvement, in four of the five studies, the respondents noted early sex experience. Hence, the respondents in the 1986 female sample first experienced sex between twelve and nineteen years of age while eighteen of the nineteen respondents in the 1986 male sample were between five and seventeen years of age when they had their first sex experience and one was twenty-one. Similarly, the respondents in the 1981 expectant teen sample experienced sex in their teen years; and four-fifths of the forty-six respondents in the 1971 study experienced sex in their teens and gave birth to their first child between age fifteen and nineteen.

Sex Experience

Though location of sex activity was not a question in earlier research, by chance we learned in both 1986 studies that parents' homes, especially those of male partners, serve as hotels for sex life. According to the respondents, homes are used as hotels in the absence of parents; however, some respondents' parents allowed them to use their homes without consideration of their presence.

Sex Participation

The respondents in the four adult studies noted several reasons for sex participation. For example, the respondents indicated that it resulted from strong sex desire, deep love for their boyfriends, low self esteem, a rebellious attitude toward parents, boyfriend and father pressure, and inadequate sex training.

Pregnancy

The respondents gave more reasons for pregnancy than sex participation. According to the 1971 female respondents, they became pregnant because their boyfriends refused to use contraception, one boyfriend failed to keep his coitus interruptus promise, and they lacked adequate contraceptive knowledge and incentive to use it, along with the need for economic assistance.

On the other hand, the 1977 adult female sample identified sex groups who contribute to single parenthood. They are mothers, grandmothers, church leaders, peers, males, and girls, themselves. For example, regarding mothers, they noted that it results from mother permissiveness, mother-daughter hostility, and mothers' encouragement, failure to talk against it, and provide sound sex education; further, it results because parents do not request school systems to add sex education courses to the curriculum. On the other hand, grandmothers encourage single parenthood by participating in the childrearing process, providing food, lodging and money, and displaying happiness over their grandchildren. Unlike mothers and grandmothers, according to the respondents, church leaders contribute to pregnancy by impregnating a girl or engaging in sex with her. When it comes to other men who raise single parenthood statistics, the respondents related that several groups of men, including boyfriends, male neighbors, boyfriends of girls' mothers, and girls' stepfathers, fathers, cousins, and uncles also cause pregnancy or help girls become sexually active that sometimes leads to pregnancy. Usually boyfriends contribute to single parenthood by attempting to create a macho image and giving girls misinformation about their fecundity and contraception while male neighbors obtain sexual favors by first giving young girls clothes and money. Then, of course, peers and personal desire for sex and children encourage single parenthood.

There are still other reasons that explain single parenthood among our people. They include, the 1986 female respondents say, birth control pills that made them sick and failure to obtain a type they could take. A related cause is that when the respondents were advised to discontinue the pill, the did not use back-up contraception. Of course, a more frequent cause for pregnancy was carelessness; respondents failed to take the pill correctly. To clarify young women's use of birth control pills, I contacted a social worker at a Norfolk Clinic and asked her to describe black girls' use of contraception. She identified four patterns: (1) when girls go to the clinic, they usually have begun sex participation, (2) often when they decide to seek help at the clinic, unbeknowing to them, they are pregnant, (3) when their menstrual cycle is delayed, for purposes other than pregnancy, the scare is enough to send them to the clinic and, (4) once they get the pill, some girls do not take it because of carelessness and a degree of unconcern about pregnancy; nonetheless, there are girls who fail to take it because they forget it. It seems apparent that taking the pill is a heavy responsibility for girls age twelve to seventeen years. They are adolescents, yet, they have an added responsibility -- using contraception on a schedule. Furthermore, poor communication between the respondents and their parents and between them and their boyfriends about birth control and a high level of communication with peers about parenthood also contributed to pregnancy.

The 1986 male sample confirmed several reasons the women gave for single parenthood. They include failure to use contraception, especially men's dislike for condoms, and poor communication about the use of contraception. Beside, the men also noted they, too, became single parents because their girlfriends gave them the impression they were using contraception; or they and sometimes their girlfriends desired a baby. Also, the men added other reasons; for example, fatherhood occurred because women's physical appearance during pregnancy enhanced some respondents self esteem; also, fatherhood resulted from the satisfaction of knowing there is someone who is part of them. Similarly, women in the 1986 sample related they felt good about carrying a baby that represented them and their boyfriend. Also, like the women in all the samples, parenthood resulted from their dislike for abortions. According to the respondents, especially an older father, an additional reason for single parenthood is female negligence; in his opinion, it is the duty of females to prevent pregnancy, because, we, and not men, are responsible for our bodies. Since this statement is not new -- instead of resisting the onus of responsibility, it is time for us to stop complaining and blaming men and accept our task, stand guard over our bodies, and not leave them to the discretion of our men.

Birthing Stages

Though the birthing stages were not determined in the 1977 female sample, it was researched in the remaining samples. In our 1971 research, when the respondents birthed children for the native and military fathers, in Norfolk, Virginia, a majority was teens, however, some of the respondents became mothers after they married and separated or divorced. On the other hand, all twenty-three of the young women in the expectant teen sample gave birth while yet teenagers. Further, twenty of the twenty-nine female respondents in the 1986 sample mothered their first child between sixteen and nineteen years of age while eight became mothers the first time between twenty and twenty-four years of age. Similarly, of the eighteen responses to this question, in the 1986 male sample, eleven respondents were between fifteen and nineteen years of age while six were age twenty to twenty-four, and one was age twenty-five when they fathered their first child.

Non-Perpetuating and Perpetuating Single Parenthood

It appears that some respondents are a part of self-perpetuating parenthood. Hence, seven of the twenty-nine mothers in the 1986 study were children of single parent families while six of the nineteen fathers, in the 1986 study, were children of single parents. Yet the primary pattern is non-perpetuating single parenthood.

Parenthood More Than Once

On the other hand, among the twenty-nine mothers, fourteen were single mothers twice or more. Similarly, nine of the nineteen fathers were fathers twice or more. Hence, almost half of the mothers and fathers were parents two or more times. When compared with intergenerational perpetuation of single parenthood, intragenerational perpetuation of single parenthood is more frequent. A source of support for this observation is the finding that the male respondents were often brother of single fathers. Hence, it is apparent that pregnancy preventions are needed for boys and girls whose siblings are single parents; preventions are also needed for non-single parents, with or without single parent siblings, because prevention of the first child seems crucial to curtailing single parenthood. Yet, it is also important to focus on single parents who have only one child because it seems that second time motherhood often occurs.

Interpersonal Relations After the Onset of Pregnancy and Parenthood

Relationship Experiences of Single Mothers

Indeed varied results of parenthood were reported by the samples. According to the 1971 sample, the single mothers experienced boyfriend denial of fatherhood, parental interference, broken relationships with the fathers of their children, weaker emotional bonds with the fathers of their children, difficulty in obtaining child support, and burdensome child care, as well as abandonment of educational goals. Also, the respondents in the 1971, 1978, and 1986 studies noted girlfriend abuse. In the 1971 and 1978 research, it was mainly emotional and economic while in the 1986 studies, it was physical, verbal, and psychological abuse. Abuse occurred in relationships with their mothers, boyfriends, and mothers of their boyfriends. Hence, single motherhood is a highly abused status.

The 1981 expectant teen sample noted additional abuse; they experienced emotional strain such as worry about their unborn child, verbal abuse from parents, and shunning by family and friends. They also experienced social strain -- deprivation of freedom -- and financial strain. However, they were continuing their public education in the school organized for girls who were mothers or in the process of becoming young mothers.

Like the 1971 and 1981 respondents, the 1986 single mothers noted several results of motherhood. Hence, their relationship with the fathers of their children is either nonexistent or weaker than before pregnancy; also, some respondents consider child support and assistance with child care love for themselves while other respondents experience hugging and kissing, but no sex. However, six of the twenty-nine respondents in the 1986 study enjoy a relatively strong relationship with the fathers of their children. On the other hand, from their perspective, we found that some mothers loved the fathers of their children less after pregnancy while others loved them more and still others did not realize a change.

109

Another result of parenthood is that respondents, when it comes to child support, experience a low level of interaction with fathers of their children, but they experience a relatively high level of interaction regarding the men's expression of love for their children. Moreover, the respondents in the five studies, experience parenthood without marriage; however, some respondents in the 1971 study also experienced parenthood in marriage. They did not get married because the men were not good choices for a husband, they did not want to sacrifice their freedom, or the men did not desire marriage, including a father who was already married. Along this line, some male respondents were not always favorable toward particular women becoming the mothers of their children.

Still another result of single parenthood in the four adult studies is that, although the men provided ephemeral economic and emotional support for their children, both types of support were negligible.

Turning next to relationships between single mothers and their mothers, in the 1986 female study, the respondents experienced varied relationships with their mothers: warmth, normal inter-action, and strained and difficult relations. In addition, these respondents experienced varied relations with their boyfriends' mothers, including absence of relations and strained, helping, and close relationships.

Relationship Experiences of Single Fathers

Similarly, in the 1986 male study, the fathers noted several results of parenthood. They include inadequate income and emotional support for their children and the mothers of their children, abandonment of girlfriends, or development of a buddy or child-caring relationship with the mothers of their children, loving and strained relations with the mothers of their children, non-marriage, added responsibility, and warmth, sarcastic, and angry relations with the mothers of their children. Moreover, in retrospect, except for two respondents, fatherhood resulted in the decision that singlehood and educational/occupa-tional achievement are preferred to single fatherhood.

Survival Strategies

The 1971 female respondents survived single parenthood with the assistance of men who served as quasi fathers and husbands.

These men helped fill the economic and emotional gap in their lives and assisted with child support, care, and rearing. On the other hand, grandparents comprised a strong support system in the 1978 study; similarly, the 1981 teen sample anticipated their parents', the parents' of their boyfriends, and their boyfriends' support. In the 1986 sample, the respondents obtained support from the government, their families, fathers of their children, and other boyfriends. On the other hand, the men in the 1986 sample experienced support from the mothers of their children and their families.

In Retrospect

Although many of the male and female respondents noted they were happy about parenthood, when we looked beneath the surface and asked whether they would repeat their lives, if given a chance, and become single parents, the responses are not only enlightening, but they help provide a deeper perspective of black, single parenthood. We found that seventeen of the nineteen men in the 1986 male study noted they would not desire to become single fathers outside marriage. Similarly, with the exception of three of the twenty-nine female respondents in the 1986 study, they also would refrain from single parenthood; and forty-five of the forty-six respondents in the 1971 study would not become single mothers. And the 1978 and 1981 samples were not asked this question. Hence, as we have concluded several times, in this book, single parenthood is not synonymous with preference for this status; in retrospect, the respondents prefer an education, job, and financial stability rather than single parenthood. Therefore, 161 respondents, a teacher-respondent, and a single mother in an additional Norfolk housing development, along with my own participation in a pregnancy prevention seminar and a child abuse seminar, clarified for this study, what it means to be a single parent. It signals burdensome responsibility, at an early age, inadequate economic resources, and broken emotional bonds with parents, fathers of one's children, and mothers of the fathers of one's children, and preference for academic and job achievement. Thus, in retrospect, single parenthood is not a desired status among the 1971 and 1986 Norfolk respondents; and the 1977 and 1981 respondents were not asked this question.

Malinowski's Principle of Legitimacy is Supported in Norfolk and Tidewater, Virgnia

Like Goode, who found that the legitimacy norm exists among blacks in the Caribbean (1960), we found that it also exists in Norfolk, Virginia. It is evident in several groups. For example, female single parents experience community gossip, parental disapproval, boyfriends' mothers' disapproval, and boyfriends' disapproval. We believe these patterns of reactions only exist because the rule of legitimacy obtains in Norfolk and Tidewater, Virginia. Similarly, it is noteworthy that there is also evidence of the legitimacy norm in the 1986 single fathers' study. Hence, apparently because the norm was violated, the men either abandoned the girls or practiced love discontinuity. Though the legitimacy norm is present in all groups identified, there is a double standard. That is, when the legitimacy norm is violated, single mothers experience greater harshness than single fathers; hence, black female sex-blood power is urgent!

Support for the Culture of Poverty Model

We found that our data somewhat support Oscar Lewis' Culture of Poverty model. Lewis emphasized the study of poverty on the family and individual level. Taking his lead, first, we provide support for the model on the individual level.

Individual Level

Starting with childbearing, we found that the motives for bearing children differ for men and women. For example, women bear children to enhance their self esteem, obtain possessions and souvenirs, vent hostility on their mothers, satisfy sex desires, carry a portion of their boyfriends during pregnancy, and conform to peer norms while men father children to prove their masculinity, observe women's figures while they are carrying their chlidren, help bring someone, a child, into the world, who is part of them, and enhance their male macho image.

Family Level

A related poverty trait is that once women give birth to children, they experience multiple types of relationships, including varied types of abuse, with the fathers of their children, their children, their mothers, and the mothers of the fathers of their children.

Another poverty trait related to parenthood, as shown in Chapter Five, is that the single father's study indicates that boys are at risk when their brothers are fathers; moreover, fathers, like some of the mothers, are fathers twice or more additional times with more than one woman as mothers of their children.

Another suggested trait in the childbearing complex is that correct contraception usage is at risk because it is a major responsibility for youth who have not yet learned to be responsible -- a situation that seems to require extensive training in responsible contraceptive usage.

Still another trait of the culture of poverty on the family level is that varied men contribute to sex and pregnancy among young blacks. They are religious leaders, male neighbors, uncles and cousins, mothers' boyfriends, stepfathers, and fathers.

Modification of the Culture of Poverty Model: Societal Perpetuation of Poverty

Subcultural/Societal Level

Based on our five single parent studies, we found that poverty on the sub-cultural/societal level is not only related to the individual's link and level of linkage in the societal institutions, which seem to place the blame for poverty entirely on the victims, but it is also related to weaknesses in the societal institutions. Together, societal and individual weaknesses compound the poverty problems of the poor. For example, we found that societal institutions, including schools, churches, and welfare departments, contribute to the culture of the poor. With respect to schools, seasonal school activities are associated with seasonal pregnancies while church leadership is known to be associated with sex and pregnancy among young church members. Regarding welfare departments, implementation of paper work, to obtain child support, results in delayed support; hence, rather than request payments from the fathers of their children, single mothers rely on public assistance. By knowing this, the welfare department inadvertently encourages black men to father children. Similarly, through their leaders and perhaps their members, churches contribute to sex and pregnancy among the young. It is not adequate to say that church leaders and church members are also human and, therefore, sex is a normal experience. It is not adequate for the church to become a safe sex haven. Hence, sex life among adults and between adults and the youth should not be a part of the churches' hidden agenda. Churches, meaning their constituents, should not contribute to sex, pregnancy, parenthood, and subsequent poverty, as noted in Chapter Three. Moreover, because institutions have not yet reached absolute moral purity, because church leaders as well as church members have difficult interpersonal relations, including family relationships, when church leaders, members, and visiting friends become emotionally linked, it likely results from a sense of being unloved. Hence, probably what the church needs to do is strengthen the spiritual bond among all church leaders and members; that is, utilize the need for love, caring, and attention to enhance a purer form of frequent association.

Further, because our data in five studies in the same poverty setting, revealed multiple patterns in all interpersonal relations and behavior, it is likely that we can find many more variations in the world wide culture of the poor. What this entails, as mentioned in Chapter Four, is raising the kinds of questions we researched, as well as others, and taking a critical look at the application of the Culture of Poverty model to large populations. Hence, we concluded that our data indicate the need to modify Lewis' Culture of Poverty model. This recommendation indicates that poverty on the subculture/societal level also involves weaknesses in the society and not only underpreparation of blacks to participate effectively in societal institutions. We believe this finding is significant to self-correcting poverty. Hence, we know that the elimination of poverty requires not only a higher achievement orientation among blacks, but it also requires more responsive and responsible societal institutions, especially, the educational institutions, welfare departments, and churches.

Self-Correcting Poverty Proposition

Our five studies indicate that the main corollary, self-perpetuating of poverty, is showing signs of refutation. One example, as noted in Chapter Four and Chapter Five, is that a relatively small percentage of the respondents in the 1986 male and female studies were born to single parents. Another indication that the culture of poverty is self-correcting is the ephemeral self-correcting poverty among poor unwed fathers. For example, there is an emerging pattern of economic and love support for children, but usually there is neither love nor economic support for the mothers of their children.

Still another indication of self-correcting poverty is support systems. For example, grandmothers and boyfriends, who serve as quasi husbands and fathers, comprise the Norfolk, single, mothers' major support systems. The support systems at least relieve the depth of poverty.

Another indication that self-perpetuating poverty can become self-correcting poverty is that only six of ninety-four respondents, in retrospect, indicated they would not become single parents, if they knew what they had experienced; instead, they would follow the educational and work ethic of the American society. Hence, even in situations that have not yet demonstrated self-correction, there is a desire for reversal of their conditions. Moreover, some of the respondents are implementing self-correcting poverty. Thus, in Chapter Two, six of the forty-four single mothers are managers and officials, in Chapter Three, twenty-three expectant teens are pursuing their high school diploma, in Chapter Four, among eleven respondents, and in our sample of approximately fifty college fathers and mothers, there is a self-correcting process operating among single male and female parents in education.

Hence, we conclude that in the same poverty setting self-correcting poverty coexists with self-perpetuating poverty. This finding suggests that attention to self-perpetuating poverty should only result from efforts to convert it to self-correcting poverty. When society changes its thinking to this perspective, the groundwork will be laid for an improved America as well as an improved black ethnic group.

Solutions to Single Parenthood

On the basis of the five studies in this work, we concluded that single parenthood is a social problem that can be solved. In this chapter, we recommend solutions to single parenthood and in Chapter Eight, we present a four pronged pregnancy

prevention model that is alternately referred to as four pregnancy prevention models.

The findings in the five chapters indicate a wide range of solutions to single parenthood. To begin, one suggestion is discussions with adults and peers in varied types of organizations
about the benefits of high morals, disinterest of males in females
after pregnancy, the menstrual cycle, conception, contraception,
and consequences of pregnancy without benefit of marriage,
and responsible contraception usage.

Another possible solution is numerous workshops, sponsored
by religious, educational, and community groups, described
in the roles that mothers, grandmothers, church leaders, males,
peers, and young women play in single parenthood and indicate
the disadvantages and solutions as described in Chapter Three.

A third suggested solution is a program for housing projects
that stresses prevention of single parenthood among high risk
girls and boys. In Norfolk, at the Hunton Young Men Christian
Association, I was an observer in Ingrid Legion's (Director
of the Eastern Virginia Pregnancy Hotline) eight week seminar
for high risk girls -- girls whose sisters are single mothers
(See Chapter Eight). Drawing on Ingrid's work, in our 1986
single fathers study, we determined that brothers of single
fathers are indeed at risk, for they sometimes become single
fathers. Hence, boys and girls in these home settings are at
risk and, therefore, perpetuate single parenthood
intragenerationally. It could be that, in Norfolk, single
parenthood is perpetuated intragenerationally more often
than intergenerationally. We found support for sibling
perpetuatoin of single parenthood from Griswold et al. (1967)
and the National Council on Illegitimacy in New York City
(Garland 1967). Hence, we recommend the development of
more pregnancy prevention programs for high risk boys and
girls, age five to seventeen, in Norfolk housing developments
(Note the program model recommended is in Chapter Eight).

A fourth suggested solution is that religious and community
groups teach black males and females to crave and implement
sperm control and sex and blood power -- sexual abstinence,
or infrequent sex, an implemented contraceptive image, and
association with members of the opposite sex who also use

sperm control and sex and blood power. This suggestion incorporates the conviction that sex power and sperm control are real power, achievable power, magnificent power! Also, an underlying impetus is that men do not want some women to become mothers of their children and they make relationships difficult between themselves and the mothers of their children to prevent marriage.

A fifth suggestion is that the community request the school system to incorporate a human sexuality seminar, in the seventh through twelfth grade, using a course syllabus modeled after the one outlined in Chapter Eight.

A six suggested solution is the organization of an Adult-Youth Pal group, in housing projects, for all boys age five to seventeen; a model is suggested in Chapter Eight.

We also suggest a seventh solution to single parenthood that involves requesting the welfare department to streamline its procedure for providing child support because many of our women are not willing to deny themselves paychecks while the department implements a slow procedure. Since our men know the welfare department is slow, since they know our women cannot or will not miss a paycheck, they have a power incentive, built into the welfare system, to father children. Our men do not wish to be reported and apprehended, nor are they difficult to find; hence, a speedy system, completed within thirty days or less, with no delay in financial assistance, would probably curtail men's willingness and desire to father children outside marriage. Once our men get committed against single parenthood, eighty-five percent of the problem is solved. Hence, the present welfare procedure is likely to encourage single mothers not to report the fathers of their children as well as encourage them to become mothers more than once; Karma supports this point in her observation that welfare makes single parenthood convenient.

Eight, we recommend that, as soon as young women determine they are becoming mothers, they report the names, addresses, and employment address of the fathers of their children to the welfare department. This will allow the department to complete the paper work before the baby is born. Hence, women should secure themselves, before the birth of their en, even when their boyfriends maintain a relationship the children are born. It could be that some men maintain relationships with their expectant girlfriends until such time as the children are born to prevent the women from reporting them. They know that after childbirth the women are likely to depend mainly on public assistance. When this practice becomes widespread, men will be reluctant to risk pregnancy because they will know they will be held responsible for the children they help bring into the world.

That finding suggests yet another solution (number nine) -- that is, we recommend that the welfare department make it difficult for able bodied women to obtain child support from the government. Such difficulty should include widespread denial so that other potential mothers will be discouraged and current mothers will refuse to become mothers more than once; moreover, parents will be more reluctant to let their children use their homes as hotels, because they, especially mothers of the girls, will become the welfare system.

Ten, we recommend that the welfare department maintain a list of employers who need employees, including domestic employers, and refer welfare applicants denied awards.

Single Parenthood, Single Motherhood, and Individual Hypotheses

Single parenthood hypotheses. To begin, single fatherhood and single motherhood are greatly influenced by sibling single parenthood. Hence, in the culture of the poor, single parenthood among male and female siblings is intragenerationally trans- mitted.

Single fatherhood is more desirable than single motherhood. It results from limited economic and child care responsibility, preference for women who have not mothered their children, and freedom to pursue other women. However, single fatherhood is also a miserable existence because men are respectively called here -- Toddler fathers -- men who do not implement the expected behavior of fatherhood and who experience enor- mous aggravation from clinging women who are the mothers of their children.

Single mothers frequently prevent men from giving their children their names; perhaps this behavior is used as a last resort to obtain a marriage license. (When motherhood begins, before women settle into pregnancy, expectant fathers should get the women to sign an agreement immediately that the child, regardless of sex, will be given the men's last names).

Single fathers have a higher pre-parent and parental self-image than single mothers.

Parental abuse is a major dimension in single parenthood. Single mothers reported that their mothers did not implement a solid sex education program; however, in all probability, the children did not allow such, because they would not communicate effectively with their parents. When children misbehave, they do not care to discuss matters with their parents, because they know there will be limited, if any, agreement. Hence, they attribute the problem to non-communicating parents when, in reality, the question concerns non-communicating children. Thus, it is hypothesized that a program aimed at elminating single parenthood should focus on effective parent-child communication, when children are violating family values and norms as well as when they have not yet done so.

Single motherhood hypotheses. On the basis of the five studies in this work and participant observation in a 1986 eight week child abuse workshop for twelve single mothers and their babies in Norfolk, Virginia, under the direction of Margaret Conothal, Ann Brown, Bertha Hathaway, Alice Butler, and Venetta Parker, and in-depth interviews with three of the single parent partici-pants, I desire to recommend the following single motherhood hypotheses.

Single motherhood is abusive. Hence, it is a miserable existence comprised of emotional, educational, and physical (inadequate household setting) deprivation, loss of boyfriend, loneliness, lack of personal freedom (time and freedom to court other men -- in some cases), and constant child-care responsibility.

Our data seem to suggest still another finding. That is, parent-hood two or more additional times appears more frequent in Norfolk than perpetuation of single parenthood intergenerationally.

Single motherhood is highly associated with birth control irresponsibility, desire to obtain a husband through a child, desire to maintain a man as one's boyfriend, desire for a baby without marriage, preference for satisfying boyfriends as opposed to one's self enhancement, burdensome childrearing tasks, abuse of one's children, deprivation of freedom, and difficult relations with parents, especially mothers, and the mothers of boyfriends. Also, it is associated with loss of boyfriend's love, traumatic experiences as one seeks to hold on to the father of one's child, loneliness, isolation, social, economic, and educational deprivation, lack of personal economic support from the father of one's child, and emotional dilemmas such as worry, sadness, and unhappiness resulting from pregnancy, parenthood, and frequent emotional and physical unavailability of the father of one's child.

Frequently, black fathers desire fewer children and dislike particular women becoming the mothers of their children.

Economic consideration of the mothers of their children is not usually a primary concern of single fathers.

There is an emerging group of black, single, non-welfare mothers.

Individual level hypothesis. Finally, we recommend two hypotheses on the individual level. It is hypothesized that the male socialization, which emphasizes too much pride to cry when hurt as a child, leads to a higher self-image among black males than the socialization of black female achieves. Also, it is hypothesized that, if black youth were taught to desire sex and power -- sexual abstinence, pride in uninterrupted menstrual cycles, infrequent sex, if at all, an unswerving implemented contraception image, and association with others who have achieved sperm control and sex and blood power, black single parenthood will become virtually non-existent.

CHAPTER SEVEN

COMPARATIVE ANALYSIS: SINGLE FATHERS AND MOTHERS

Introduction

Drawing on findings in Chapters Four and Five, this chapter compares single fathers and mothers in Norfolk, Virginia in 1986. Starting with Tables 1 and 2, this analysis is begun with the background characteristics of both study populations. They include the respondents' age, parents' marital status at the time of their birth, age at time of first sex experience, age of first sex partner, age at birth of first child, number of own children, and number of opposite sex parents per respondent. As a footnote to the introduction, the male/female respondents in Chapter Four and Five were not linked; instead, they were allied with other single mothers and single fathers respectively.

Background Characteristics: Single Mothers and Single Fathers

Beginning with age, we found that the average age of the single fathers is twenty-five years while the mothers' average age is 24. Hence, age-wise the male and female samples are almost evenly matched. However, we found a larger gap between the two populations regarding age at time of first sex experience. For example, the average age of the fathers was thirteen while the average age of the mothers was sixteen. Therefore, the women began their sex life three years later than the fathers. Yet, the average age of the fathers' first sex partner was thirteen while the average age of the mothers' first sex partner was nineteen. Still on the matter of age, the average age of the fathers and mothers when they became parents the first time was nineteen. Similarly, the fathers and mothers had an average of two children each and both had the same average number of parents of their children of the opposite sex (1.5). These data indicate that the samples age-wise are similar in the demonstration of this set of traits.

121

TABLE 1. Community Single Mothers
Norfolk, Virginia, 1986

Case no	Age	Parents' marital status	Age: first sex experience	Age: first sex partner	Age: birth of first child	No of own children	No of fathers of children
1	29	single	18	20	21	4	3
2	22	single	14	21	19	2	1
3	23	married	18	19	19	1	1
4	22	married	17	19	17	2	1
5	35	married	18			3	2
6	16	single	13	16	16	1*	1
7	38	married	15	17	18	3	3
8	34	married	18	22	21	2	2
9	21	married	17	19	18	2	2
10	18	married	16	19	17	1	1
11	41	married	17	20	18	8	3
12	31	single	17	18	18	3	3
13	25	single	17	17	23	1	1
14	21	married	17	17	20	1	1
15	27	married	16	20	18	4	1
16	19	married	15	15	16	3	2
17	21	married	17	17	22	1*	1
18			16	20	17	1	1
19	17	single	15	17	17	1*	1

(Continued on next page)

122

Case no	Age	Parents' marital status	Age: first sex experience	Age: first sex partner	Age: birth of first child	No of own child-ren	No of fathers of children
20	27	married	19	24	24	1	1
21	20	married	13	28	20	1	1
22	18	married	16	18	17	1	1
23	17	married	16	17	17	1*	1
24	22	married	16	21	16	4**	3
25	19	married	12	12	17	2	2
26	23	married	17	22	17	1	1
27	23	single	16	21	23	1	1
28	27	single	13	14	19	2	1
29	19	married	15	16	18	1	1

* Expecting first child

** 1 child deceased

TABLE 2. COMMUNITY SINGLE FATHERS
Norfolk, Virginia, 1986

Case no	Age	Parents' marital status	Age: first sex experience	Age: first sex partner	Age: birth of first child	No of own children	No of fathers of children
1	17	Married	13	16	14	1	1
2	19	Single	14	15	15	1	1
3	21	Single	10	8	16	1	1
4	21	Married	13	13	21	1	1
5	22	Married	17	19	19	2	1
6	23	Married	13	14	23	1	1
7	23	Married	9	8	18	2	2
8	23	Married	5	12	19	3	1
9	23	Married	16	16	18	4	4
10	23	Married	11	13	15	1	1
11	24	Single	12	10	22	1	1
12	25	Single	12	12	--	2	2
13	26	Married	13	13	24	1	1
14	27	Married	14	14	26	2	2
15	30	Single	13	12	15	4	2
16	30	--	15	12	20	4	3
17	32	Married	13	14	18	1	1
18	41	Single	15	17	17	5	2
19	--	Married	14	11	21	1	1

Further analysis of the age specific data revealed additional comparisons between the fathers and mothers. For example, based on Table 1 and Table 2, we found that the most dangerous teen years for single community men were age fifteen and eighteen (three births each year) followed by age nineteen (two births each year) and twenty-one (two births each year). Hence, the men were more likely to become fathers at these ages than any other time. On the other hand, the most dangerous years for the women were seventeen (eight births at that age) and eighteen (six births) followed by age sixteen and nineteen (three births each year). These findings indicate that from age fifteen, the teens were the high risk years for both sexes, a finding consistent with Norfolk teen mothers (See Chapter One).

Also, we compared the education of the respondents. The mothers are more highly educated than the men (See Chapter Four and Chapter Five). For example, fifteen (78.9 percent) of the nineteen fathers had obtained seven to twelve years of education while twenty-one (72.4 percent) of twenty-nine mothers had received between ten and twelve years of education. Unlike the fathers, eleven mothers are in the process of correcting their education. Hence, when the process is complete, the gap between the sexes will be enhanced. Another finding is that twice as many men as women are employed. It follows that the women depended more heavily than the men on public assistance and support from the fathers of their children or boyfriends than employment.

Poverty Traits: Single Mothers and Single Fathers

Subcultural, Communal, Family and Individual Level

Turning to Oscar Lewis' Culture of Poverty model, we utilized Chapter Four and Chapter Five to compare the support provided the model by the Norfolk single mothers and Norfolk single fathers. Beginning with the subcultural/societal level, as noted in Table 3 and Table 4, there is considerable support. Single parents of both sexes demonstate the same traits, however, single mothers seem to have more cash than single fathers. What this probably suggests is that single fathers are friendly with two or three women, including the mothers of their children, who share their public assistance checks. If this reasoning

TABLE 3. Poverty Traits and Related Indicators
Among Black Single Mothers
Norfolk, Virginia, 1986

Level	Indicators	Number of mothers
Subcultural/ societal level		
Residential separation	Separate housing developments	29
Housing Support	Subsidized housing	29
Education	10th-12th grade	21
Employment	No job	20
Low Income	Low paying jobs	9
Chronic shortage of cash	ADC, WIC, low wages	29
Communal level		
Poor Housing	Public housing	29
Crowding	Young Park-1578 bedrooms, 750 families; Calvert Park, 666 bedrooms, 312 families	29
Place of social contacts	Social behavior confined to courtyards, friends' homes, stores, and the streets (places of entertainment)	29
Interpersonal relations	Confined to fathers of children, children, family, peers, boyfriends' mothers	29

(Continued on next page)

126

Level	Indicators	Number of mothers
Family level		
Mother-daughter talk (in childhood)	None	11
Birth control	None at time of conception	27
Single parenthood	None married either the father of their children or another male	29
First reactions to the onset of motherhood	Happiness	7
Mother-respondent relations after onset of motherhood	Happiness or normal relations	5
Grandmother-respondent relations after onset of motherhood	Happiness	3
Current relations with mothers of boyfriends	None	7
Absence of childhood as a specially prolonged and pro-protected stage	Began sex interaction between age 12-19	29
	Early childbearing (between 16-19)	20
Location of sex	Homes of respondents or boyfriends	9
Level of communication, with father of child, before onset of parenthood about their futures	None	24

(Continued on next page)

Level	Indicators	Number of mothers
Emotional relationship with bofriend at beginning pregnancy	Young man was not respondents favorite boyfriend	6
Abandonment (None/very little contact)	Beginning pregnancy or after child birth	9
Child support	None	18
	Vague	8
Perpetuation of single parenthood	Respondents' mothers were single parents	8
	Two or three men fathered a respondent's children	10
	Mothers twice or more	14
Individual level		
Helplessness	Fathers of children underequipped to provide child support	18
Respondents' boyfriends	underequipped to provide them with economic support	29
	Boyfriends are under-prepared to maintain a strong relationship (after the onset of pregnancy or birth)	23
Inferiority	Loved boyfriends more during pregnancy because they had a part of the men inside them	6
	The respondents developed a sense of love through child support	11

(Continued on next page)

Level	Indicators	Number of mothers
	Wanted first baby at time of conception	8
	Honored boyfriends' request for a baby	8
Dependence	Underprepared to earn a good living (9 are employed in low-paying occupations)	29

* Church attendance was not determined.

TABLE 4. Poverty Traits and Related Indicators
Among Black Single Fathers
Norfolk, Virginia, 1986

Level	Indicators	Number of Mothers
Subcultural/ societal level		
Residential separation	Separate housing developments	19
Education	7th-12th grade	15
Employment	No job	6
Low Income	Low paying jobs	5
Chronic shortage of cash	6 no jobs, 5 low paying jobs	11
Communal level		
Inadequate Housing	Live with parents/mothers in subsidized housing	
Crowding	Young/Calvert Park as noted in Table 3	19
Interpersonal relations Family level	Same as females in Table 3	19
Father-son talk (in childhood)	None/or not much 6 plus 5 fathers who deceased early	11
Birth control	None at time of conception	19
Single parenthood	None married the mother of their children or other females	19

(Continue on next page)

Level	Indicators	Number of Mother
First reactions to the onset of fatherhood	Happiness, joy, enjoyment	8
Absence of childhood as a specially prolonged and protected stage	Initial sex experience was between age 5 and 18, one excepted	18
Level of communication, with mother of child, before onset of parenthood about their futures	Poor, low, or deceptive	7
Emotional relationship with girlfriend at beginning pregnancy	Young man was not respondents favorite boyfriend	4
Child support	None	8
Perpetuation of single parenthood	Respondents' mothers were single parents	6
	Fathers twice or more	9
	More than one mother of children	9
Individual level ----------------		
Helplessness	Underprepared to support child and mother	19
Inferiority	Loved girlfriends more during pregnancy because they were carrying a part of them in their stomachs	7
	Chose not to use contraception	12
	Wanted first child at time of conception	11
Dependence	Unemployed	6

is accurate, perhaps single mother support for men leads to greater poverty than they would ordinarily experience. We thus conclude that single, motherhood poverty on the subcultural/societal level is aided and abetted by unemployed black men.

The Norfolk respondents also support the model on the communal level. Hence, single mothers and fathers experience poor housing, crowded living conditions, and limited participation in the social, political, and financial institutions in the city (See Table 3 and Table 4).

Moreover, the respondents support the culture of poverty on the family level. As shown in Table 3 and Table 4, on the family level, the single parent experiences are similar, but there are some differences. For example, proportionally speaking, the Norfolk single fathers perpetuated single parenthood intergenerationally more often than the single mothers. Another major difference between single mothers and single fathers is that single mothers provide more child support that single fathers; although the women receive public assistance, it is their duty to implement and perpetuate the process of receiving help while men are disassociated from the process. Also, a larger proportion of the single fathers than single mothers desired their first child at time of conception. Though these differences exist between single fathers and single mothers, Table 3 and Table 4 note considerable support for the culture of poverty.

Similarly, the respondents provide support on the individual level. For example, as indicated in Table 3, it appears that the women, more so than the fathers of their children, were able to sustain an emotional relationship following pregnancy. When this finding is coupled with the finding on the family level that single mothers are more responsible than single fathers for child support, among other findings in Chapter Five, we concluded that single fathers' self-image is more positive than single mothers' self-image; that is, the single fathers have not placed themselves under as much stress as single mothers. Assuming this point to be accurate, we propose that improvement in the self-image of young girls will impede the single parenthood trend.

Norfolk Single Mothers and Single Fathers: Self-Correcting Poverty

Our findings also indicate that single parents are correcting poverty on the subculture level. Specifically, the 1986 studies of single mothers and single fathers in Norfolk indicate that self-correcting poverty co-exist in the same setting with self-perpetuating poverty. As noted in Table 5 and Table 6, there are several indications of self-correcting poverty. Also, there is some indication of variation in the process, by sex of single parent. Hence, on the subcultural level, our findings indicate that Norfolk single mothers were more likely than single fathers to continue their education following single parenthood. On the other hand, a larger proportion of the single fathers than single mothers is employed. As a result of these findings, we concluded that single mothers are making more progress correcting poverty through education while single fathers are making more progress correcting poverty through employment; and both sexes, though not enough, indicate self-correcting poverty.

On the family level, there is additional evidence of self-correcting poverty by sex of single parent. For example, a larger proportion of the female than male respondents became parents of children by their favorite boyfriend or girlfriend. Similarly, a larger proportion of the men than women perpetuated single parenthood. Concerning continuation of love, our data are incomplete, however, there is a very slight indication of post-pregnancy love.

Also, on the individual level, the single mothers and single fathers are similar when it comes to self-correcting poverty. For example, usually conception occurred in a favorite relationship with the opposite sex. Yet, the single fathers were more favorable than the single mothers toward single parenthood. Perhaps, most important is that, in retrospect, both sexes prefer not to be parents. A related finding is that love for children is not the same as desiring single motherhood and single fatherhood status. Clearly, the respondents love their children, yet they noted that single parenthood is not their preferred status. This finding suggests that it is incumbent upon the family, community, state, and nation, to help youth become convinced that though single parenthood may look attractive, after the fact, it is not desired.

TABLE 5. Self-Correcting Poverty Traits
         and Related Indicators Among
         Black Single Mothers
         Norfolk, Virginia, 1986

Level	Indicators
Subcultural/societal	
Self-correcting education	Continuation of education: Completion of high school, community college, vocational school. Eleven respondents are correcting or have lessened the impact of motherhood on their education
Self-correcting employment	Nine respondents are employed
Family	
Single parenthood occurs in favorite boyfriend relations	Twenty three respondents became mothers for men who were their favorite boyfriends
Non-repetitive motherhood	15 respondents
Single fathers' child care behavior	boyfriends are daily or weekend fathers
Maintained the love of their boyfriends	6 respondents
Individual	
Attitudes toward pregnancy	Mainly unhappiness; others were happiness or mixed emotions
Motherhood is different from preference for the status	Though the respondents love their children, only 3 of 29 noted it as their preferred status
In retrospect	26 respondents noted they preferred a better education, job, housing, and children after marriage; also, they indicated that abstinence or contraception would be implemented if they could start over with what they know.

TABLE 6. Self-Correcting Poverty Traits and Related
          Indicators Among Black Single Fathers
          Norfolk, Virginia, 1986

Level	Indicators
Subcultural/societal	
Employment	13 respondents are employed
Income	5 Respondents earn between $1200 and $3,000 monthly
Family	
Single parenthood occurs in favorite girlfriend relationship	13 of 17 respondents fathered children in favorite girlfriend relationship
Born to married parents	12 of 18 respondents
Continued to love girlfriend after she mothered child	of 10 respondents queried, four get along together; two appear happy
Individual	
Attitudes toward pregnancy	Of the 18 responding, 3 were neutral, seven disappointed
Fatherhood is different from preference for fatherhood status	17 of 19 respondents prefer singlehood without parenthood
In retrospect	17 respondents prefer employment, only one mother of their children, improved education, contraceptive usage, assignment of their last names to their children, virginity until marriage, and marriage before parenthood

Thus, Chapters Four and Five and Tables 5 and 6 note that self-correcting poverty is in progress in the same setting as self-perpetuating poverty. This finding seems significant because it indicates the solvability of poverty; consequently, we can choose to spend more time solving the problem than condemning societal institutions and victims.

Single Mothers and Fathers: Comparison of Interpersonal Relations

<u>Causes of Single Parenthood</u>

Beside background characteristics, contributions to self-perpetuating poverty, and contributions to self-correcting poverty, the findings indicate comparisons of single mothers' and single fathers' interpersonal relations. Because of its significance, we begin this comparison with the birth status of the respondents. We found that a larger percentage of the mothers (71) than fathers (67) was born to married parents (See Table 1 and Table 2). This finding seems to indicate that relatively high percentages of the respondents initiated rather than perpetuated single parenthood and that factors other than single parent households are at work in making single parents. Hence, the single mothers and fathers are similar in that self-perpetuating poverty is not their primary trait.

Based on this finding, further data analysis indicates that several other traits, some heretofore uncited in the literature, account for single fatherhood and single motherhood. Also, the findings indicate both overlap and differences in interpersonal relationships that led to single motherhood and single fatherhood.

Judging by the five studies, we concluded that, among single mothers, such factors as rebellion against parents who strive to insulate their children against a burdensome youth and young adulthood, public assistance availability, dislike for male contraception, carelessness in using female contraception, unconcern about the outcome of sexual activity, peer influence, low female self-esteem, female love for men more so than themselves, male-self love rather than love for women, lack of enough pride to maintain sex and blood power, weakness of personality that prevents one from deferring the ultimate in sexual gratification, and acquiesence to sexual and baby requests are major contributions to single motherhood.

136

Moreover, women as the four studies have shown, sometimes bear children to obtain husbands or maintain the love of their boyfriends. In effect, the very act of mothering leads to love discontinuity; also, it results in some women sharing only a caretaking relationship with the father of her child.

On the other hand, based on Chapter Five, rather than perpetuation of their birth status, usually birth to married parents, the men became single fathers because they disregarded parental pleas and warnings, delighted in the disfigurement of women, desired a child because it is part of themselves, desired ego-enhancement through female, self-sacrifice and detriment, courted women who failed to manage their bodies and implement contraceptive usage, derived happiness from using sweet talk and kindness to influence women to risk pregnancy, complied with females' request for a baby, the public assistance department required enormous paper work before locating them, dislike for condoms, girlfriends dislike for male contraception, and desire for sexual pleasure.

Chapters Four and Five also noted reasons for single motherhood and single fatherhood. Thus, there are some reasons for single parenthood that are attributed to both sexes. For example, as noted earlier, the desire to obtain a possession, a child, without concern for the impact of single parenthood on that life accounted for single parenthood. A child born out of wedlock is placed under a heavy burden that he/she carries the remainder of their lives. Therefore, single parents demonstrate a degree of inconsideration for the helpless, the child. They think only about themselves -- hence, their personality is somewhat incomplete. That is, their emotions and behavior should take into consideration the young child's life who is born to parents with inadequate social status; inadequate resources, inadequate material things, inadequate love, inadequate family structure. Beside, the children often come up in a setting where their financial support is a funding agency; since the breadwinning role in the American family is expected to be the father's responsibility, though the mother may assist, it does not appear that non-provider men are socially entitled to be called fathers. We do know, however, that a few pregnancies come from lack of knowledge, but in 1986, there is no excuse for contraceptive iliteracy. As we found in the Norfolk clinic described earlier and in the five studies, carelessness, on the part of single mothers and single fathers, in using birth control and dislike for condoms also lead to pregnancy In effect, contraceptive carelessness suggests that the women and men are not sufficiently concerned about women's bodies and lives.

Solvability of Single Parenthood

These data-based causes of single fatherhood and single mother-hood can be solved with an organized and concentrated nation-wide effort. What we need to do is teach a new sex orientation a new view of the person, and enhanced interpersonal, cross-sex relations, which at first will resemble a foreign language but once learned, lives will be happier, more successful, and highly enthusiastic, the race will be more prideful, and America will realize perpetually accruing funds that once were used to support perpetually accruing single parenthood. Intervention models that seek to reorganize the lives of youth and refurbish the black family, are described in Chapter Eight.

Respondent and Parental Relations and Single Mothers and the Mothers of the Fathers of Their Children

Further, concerning interpersonal relations, we also compared mother-daughter and father-son talk. What we found is that eleven of the twenty-nine mothers did not engage in girls talk with their mothers while six of the nineteen fathers had not experienced boys' talk with their own fathers. Though neither sample received a solid sex education, a majority of the parents attempted to spare them the ordeal of single parent-hood. Judging by the sex education comments, parents were as effective as they knew how to be; because they did not realize the success they so often desired, it appears that preg-nancy prevention needs a quadruple pronged prevention as outlined in Chapter Eight. This means that families need help from the entire community and we hope these studies will promote greater community awareness that single parenthood is not only a family or race problem, but it is a community state, and national problem, yet the black family, black race and black individual must never relinquish their input in success-fully bringing up their children; that is, families must not hold the community responsible for childrearing, instead, they must join hands with the community in bringing up their children

A feeling of closeness between the community and families can improve interpersonal relations and accomplish an achieving generation among the poorest of the poor.

Our findings indicate additional relationships, including first reaction to the onset of first pregnancy, between the respondents and the other parent of their children. When we compared the reactions of the females' mothers with those of the males' mothers to their forthcoming parenthood, we also found similarities (See Chapter Four and Chapter Five). The female respondents experienced warm, normal, strained, and difficult relations with their mothers while the male respondents experienced mother-resignation to their single parenthood, sarcasm, and anger.

A similar comparison is the relationship between the respondents and the mothers of their boyfriends or girlfriends (See Chapter Four). Of the female respondents asked about their relationship with the mothers of the fathers of their children, seven reported no relationship while eleven reported varied patterns, including closeness and helping relations. This question was not pursued as consistently in the men's study, but the experiences of the women are consistent with those in Atlanta, Georgia, married relationships (Barnes 1981:369-374).

Respondents and The Parents of Their Children

Another comparison between the single mothers and single fathers concerns contraceptive usage. We found that twenty seven of the twenty-nine female respondents did not use birth control; yet, seven of the nineteen men believed their girlfriends were using contraception and were disappointed with pregnancy. We found that one female was deceived by a boyfriend, but seven males were deceived by their girlfriends. The message in this finding seems to be that deception by both boyfriends and girlfriends leads to single parenthood.

Another interpersonal relations comparison is first reaction to the onset of pregnancy. (See Chapter Four and Chapter Five). Among the women, seven were happy, six had mixed emotions, and ten were unhappy while eight men expressed happiness, enjoyment, and joy, three were neutral, and seven were disappointed. Proportionally speaking, the men were more disappointed with single parenthood than the women. This finding seems to indicate that the single fathers have a more positive self-image than the single mothers. A related finding is that some of the women became pregnant out of love for their boyfriends and to please them; yet, as noted earlier, the very act of trying to please the men led to broken relationships. Similar to the previous finding, it appears again that the men have a more positive image of themselves than the women. Still another related finding is that four of the fathers did not desire the mothers of their children to bear children for them, but no comparable finding was noted in the women's data. Perhaps this is additional support for the observation that men who become single fathers have a higher self-image than women who become single mothers. On the basis of our findings about the male and female respondents, we have concluded that black men have a higher positive self image than black females -- a serious cause for single parenthood. It keeps the men from marrying women who are mothers before marriage, it encourages them to bear children to prove that women will bow to their requests, probably a rich source of pride -- a sense of achievement. That is, we believe that child-bearing is not only to receive a possession, but to get someone, their girlfriend, to perform an act that shows self-sacrifice and leaves a detrimental life-time mark on her life in honor of the man she thought loved her. Also, we concluded that the male socialization process builds a more positive self-image than the female socialization process. What we mean, for example, is that when boys are told not to cry, even when they are hurting, this encourages them to think well of themselves; it encourages them to abide by the rule -- no crying -- an achievement that leads them to think they are too strong and important to cry. On the other hand, the female socialization process that encourages crying weakens the self-image because we are allowed to feel hurt and deprived. This crying phenomenon radiates into adult types of behavior that leaves many women with a relatively low self image. If our perception is correct, this pattern is not confined to any one race; moreover, it may be worthwhile to educate girls away from crying and feeling helpless -- which probably enhances their sense of inferiority -- while growing up -- to a sense of personality sufficiency and self-respect.

We also compared child support (See Chapter Four and Five). The women overwhelmingly are responsible for child support.

For instance eighteen of the women noted that the fathers of their children do not provide child support, yet all respondents contribute to the economic support of their children, even if it only includes dealing with public assistance offices which can be an arduous, demeaning, time consuming, and annoying task. Similarly, eight of the fathers in this study noted they do not provide child support. And in both samples the fathers show their children more love than they provide child support. This also entails fathers serving as daily and weekend fathers while women are on perpetual call, if not duty. Hence, single motherhood is even more burdensome than fatherhood in caring for their children.

Concerning love, as noted in Chapter Four and Chapter Five, both samples indicated they loved their boyfriend or girlfriend more during pregnancy. The reason the women loved the fathers of their children more was because they were carrying inside them a part of the men while the men loved the mothers of their children more during pregnancy because the women were carrying a part of them. Hence, both sexes built their self-esteem on the nine month period -- mainly to the disadvantage of the women. Following the birth of the child, love in both samples usually dissipated and none married the fathers of their children. Though a few of the men enjoy the mothers of their children other respondents find relations with the mothers of their children unpleasant or discontinued. Another area of interpersonal comparison concerns reasons for not getting married. The women noted they did not marry the fathers of their children because they did not want to curtail their freedom, neither they nor their boyfriends were ready for marriage, and the men would not make good marriage partners. On the other hand, the male respondents did not marry the mothers of their children because they considered marriage too much responsibility, desired to preserve their freedom, the women were unfaithful, they did not love them enough for marriage, preferred women who were not mothers, and a grandmother, incarceration, and financial instability prevented it.

As indicated in Chapter Four and Chapter Five, when we compared what the respondents would do in retrospect, with their knowledge of single parenthood, the samples were almost identical. Hence, only two of the nineteen fathers and three of the twenty-nine mothers would repeat single parenthood. We thus concluded that parental love for children does not bespeak the deeper desire of the male/female respondents -- single parenthood is not, in our samples, synonymous with the desired life status.

To conclude, our comparison of single fathers and mothers in Norfolk indicates that single parenthood is complex and requires family and community cooperation for its solution. Further, we conclude that the Norfolk fathers demonstrate a higher positive self-image than the Norfolk females. With this conclusion, we recommend that the socialization of the women be modified to include the factors that promote a high self image and that the male socialization process be amended to include more sensitivity toward the care of women. A more well-rounded and similar socialization process will probably contribute to fewer black single mothers and fathers in Norfolk.

CHAPTER EIGHT

MODELS FOR PREGNANCY PREVENTION

Introduction

Our goal has been to determine the background and experiences of black, single fathers and mothers in Norfolk and Tidewater, Virginia. This information was obtained to: (1) determine whether Malinowski's Principle of Legitimacy obtains in Norfolk, Virginia, (2) provide support for the culture of poverty, (3) suggest additions to the culture of poverty, (4) propose a Self-Correcting Poverty proposition, (5) provide solutions to single motherhood and single fatherhood, (6) provide data-based single parenthood hypotheses for further research, (7) compare single mothers with single fathers and, (8) develop a data-based four pronged pregnancy prevention model, alternately referred to as four pregnancy prevention models.

Single Parenthood Prevention Models

Judging by the many actors in the single parenthood complex, we decided that a multiple pronged model is needed to bring single parenthood under control. However, based on our findings, we also believe that either model used independently will reap valuable benefits. Our first prong focuses on concerned youth and adults for pregnancy prevention.

Youth Advocates for Singlehood Without Parenthood Model

This model is provided by Ingrid E. Ligeon, Eastern Virginia Pregnancy Hotline, the Family Planning Council, Norfolk, Virginia. The council's plan not only has an interesting history, but it is also successfully implemented in Norfolk. This plan for preventing adolescent pregnancies centers around a young woman's concern for the youth of our region. Ingrid's background is relevant to her pregnancy prevention work. She stated:

When I arrived in the USA from Surinam, I had always said, this is my chance to make something of my life and give back what I reap. Well, since becoming a naturalized citizen, many opportunities have come my way and thank God I was and am able to take advantage of them all. Working with adolescents from various communities has been a fulfilling experience. For the past year, I have had the opportunity to work with several groups. The one that is most relevant to this book about single parents is Team Counsel. It has a membership of twenty young ladies who decided that learning about life-coping skills was an immediate necessity. The group decided that adolescent pregnancy prevention would be their prime focus.

Ingrid, an employee at the Norfolk Planning Council, and Helen Epstein, a Norfolk State University Master of Social Work student intern and twenty young ladies age 5 to 17 conduct this program.

The model has four components.

Component Number 1

One element in pregnancy prevention is weekly class instruction. Ingrid conducts the training program around six topics:

Know Your Body

Say No, the Best Form of Birth Control

Family Planning

Self Esteem

Goal Setting

Careers

In these sessions, Ingrid and Helen are able to get the young girls to describe their social life with young men and retrain them. They rely heavily on the girls to answer questions, make comments, and develop internal convictions to follow the rules of pregnancy prevention and wholesome boy-girl relationships.

I was privileged to be an observer in these sessions. Ingrid is a young woman, who knows how to talk with youth, age five to seventeen, and get them to reveal almost everything they do socially. After self revelation, Ingrid skillfully changes their thinking about boy-girl relationships, in the same session, without them realizing what she is doing. Helen, like Ingrid, is interested and personable and makes a valuable contribution to Team Counsel. Because both young women convey love, warmth, and caring, in turn, Ingrid, Helen and the girls comprise a strong group of advocates for singlehood without motherhood.

Component Number 2

Ingrid and Helen have trained the young girls to serve as advocates in the community for pregnancy prevention. Their team life goes beyond the Hunton YMCA where the training sessions are held. It extends to joint television appearances, newspaper interviews, and testimonies before committees concerned with teenage pregnancy. Ingrid wrote:

> It was during our session on Family Planning that Team Counsel members decided to become advocates in the community issues that deal with prevention programs. These young ladies have testified before the subcommittee studying teenage pregnancy in the Commonwealth of Virginia (HJR61) with great expertise. After all, they, too, are teenagers.

The team counsel members also became involved in the school based clinic issues. As Ingrid notes:

> The Team Counsel members expressed their views on comprehensive school based clinics in that memorable Norfolk School Board hearing October 28, 1986. The school board voted unanimously to give the Norfolk Health Department space in a local high school to implement a comprehensive clinic. I truly believe that because of the stand taken by thirteen and fourteen year old adolescents, the adults in Norfolk, Virginia are beginning to open their eyes.

The Team Counsel members have just begun their work in educating the public. They realize adolescent pregnancy is a problem and are advocating for prevention programs.

Component 3

It appears that adults are listening to the dedicated Team Counsel. This observation is supported by Ingrid's initiation of a mothers' group for the purpose of teaching them how to talk with their daughters. As the findings throughout this book note, mother-daughter hostility often leads to single parenthood. Hence, successful parental training is likely to enhance family relations as well as prevent single motherhood. Ingrid's first meeting with a group of mothers was held November 17, 1986. While visiting my office the day of the meeting, Ingrid was jubilant about the opportunity to help mothers learn to deal effectively with their adolescent daughters.

Component Number 4

On the basis of my participant observation in the Team Counsel's sessions and child bonding sessions for young mothers, conducted by a multi-racial group, we highly recommend that women of all races, religions, and ethnic groups cooperate in pregnancy prevention programs for all teens, especially blacks, since the problem has such widespread proportions in black communities.

We highly recommend the Family Planning Council's model. With youth talking to adults and other youth about pregnancy prevention, we may be able to reverse single parenthood. Moreover, if several young women in a city without regard for color, race, or religion, work to curtail adolescent pregnancy, single pregnancy and infant mortality rates are likely to decrease. Perhaps it should be mentioned that the Team Counsel's program is housed in the Virginia National Bank and supported by the Norfolk citizenry. Though adolescent pregnancy is mainly a black social problem, we need the assistance of the entire city.

Human Sexuality Training in Schools: Seventh through Twelfth Grade Model

Our first recommendation is the formation of a Concerned Citizens Campaign for Youth to request the school board in each Tidewater city to implement a course entitled, An Agenda for Human Sexuality, to be taught, starting the first semester of junior high school and ending the second semester of the twelfth grade, using the following syllabus, with appropriate adaptation and addenda for each grade level.

An Agenda for Human Sexuality

I.   Course Content: Literature Based

A.   Menstruation, Contraception, and Impregnation

B.   Male Fecundity

C.   Male Contraceptive Information

D.   School Activities that Lead to Sex and Pregnancy

E.   Female Sex and Blood Power

F.   Sex and Blood Power Pride

G.   Constant Use of Schools' Birth Control Clinics

H.   Effective Techniques for Dealing with Hostility Toward Parents

I.   Significance of Scholastic and Character Achievement

J.   Significance of Common Sense, Deferred Sex-Gratification, and Charming Dispositions At and Away From Home

K.   Importance of Jobs for Male and Female Teens and Emphasis on Female Refusal of Monetary Gifts from Men

L.   Male Orientation Toward Sex

M.   Male Orientation Toward News of Forthcoming Fatherhood

N.   Males Loose Love for Girlfriends Who Become Mothers of Their Children

O.   Single Mother Verbal, Physical, and Emotional Abuse

P.   Failure of Single Motherhood to Obtain Marriage License

Q.   Male Church Leaders and Teen Sex and Pregnancy

R.   Male Neighbors and Sex With Young Girls

S.   Older Women, Young Boys, and Sex

T.   Older Men, Young Men, and Sex

U.   Fathers, Stepfathers, Relatives, and Sex with Young Girls

V.   Male Self Esteem

W.   Female Self Esteem

(Also, we suggest a strong Dating/Courting for Success unit. Suggested topics are types of deception in male/female relations, the importance of quality (satisfying) male/female relations (not including sex), the life time disadvantages to children born in unwed unions, the burdensome nature of single parenthood, especially to mothers, the ways children born out of wedlock interfere with life goals, the disappointing nature of single parenthood immediately after the onset of pregnancy or childbirth, cues that a man is thinking about making a woman the mother of a child -- the cue abstracted from out data is that children become a discussion topic in their relations -- however, the timing of these children in these discussions is after marriage, which often never takes place, a process that sometimes leaves women unsuspecting. Men rarely maintain their promise to marry girls if they become pregnant, and men prefer women who do not mother their children.)

II.   Class Activities: Panel Discussion Topics

A.   "If You Loved Me, You Would"

B.   "If you Don't I'm Going to Quit You"

C. If you Loved Me and Yourself, you Would Not Ask
    Me to Engage in Sex

D. If you Loved Me and Yourself, You Would Not Want
    to Risk Pregnancy and Our Future

E. Female Sex and Blood Power

F. Male Sex Power and Sperm Control Power

G. The Possibility That Men Usually Don't Love Women
    In Sex Alliances (Courtship)

H. The Male Socialization Process that Emphasizes
    the James Bond and John Wayne Types Contribute
    to a More Positive Male Image than the Female
    Socialization Process

I. Money, Sex and Pregnancy

J. The Reactions and Consequences of Pregnancy
    for Young Girls (Biologically, Socially, Emotionally,
    Educationally, and Occupationally - Also, Invite
    Positive Speakers to Share Their Experiences to
    Reinforce the seriousness of single parenthood)

III. Class Activities: Term Paper Followed by Class Discussions

A. Single Parents' Panel Discussion (Invited Guest
    or Class Members, if Present)

B. Male/Female Panel Discussion on each Subtopic
    in the Syllabus

C. Term Paper: How and Why I Guard My Sexuality

D. Term Paper: Why I Use Sex Power

E. Term Paper: I Tell my Friends That My Parents
    Don't Communicate With Me; Actually, It Is The
    Other Way Around. I Don't Commuicate With Them
    Because I am Violating Our Family Values and
    Teachings.

149

F.   Panel Discussion on Parental Abuse

G.   Panel Discussion on Single Mother Abuse From Their Mothers

H.   Panel Discussion on Single Mother Abuse From Their Boyfriends

I.   Types of male/female deception

J.   The Beneficial Results of Honest Male/Female Relations

K.   Quality (beside sex) interpersonal male/female relations

L.   The life-time disadvantages of single parenthood on the child born outside marriage

Beside schools, we recommend that the Concerned Citizens For Youth Group also attempt to get this suggested course implemented by churches, civic groups, and Greek Letter organizations. It would be especially appropriate for christian education departments in churches, youth work in civic groups, and educational programs in Greek Letter organizations.

Parental Model for Improving Family Relations and Pregnancy Prevention

This model also involves churches, civic groups, Greek Letter organizations, and PTAs. It is recommended that they sponsor parent seminars using the following title and syllabus:

Parental Agenda for Child Rearing

A.   Child Disciplining Techniques for Rearing Children and Maintaining Family Unity

B.   Parent-Child Dialogue Techniques for Maintaining and Improving Parent-Child Behavior

C.   Effective Mother-Daughter/Son Dialogue When Children are Heavy into Violating Family Norms

150

and Values and When They Still are Abiding by
Family Rules

D.   Parental Listening

E.   How to Teach Sex Education at Home

F.   Do's and Don'ts for Grandmothers

It appears that the type of education suggested here is necessary
to stem the tide of single parenthood and improve family unity.
Hence, we ask that the schools, PTAs, churches, civic groups,
and Greek Letter organizations make a difference by implementing the suggested syllabi, because they seek to educate
the social, economic, and moral self -prerequisites for containing
single parenthood and maintaining students in the public schools.

Home Sex Education: Fatherhood Prevention

Pals for Black Manhood Program

1.   Youth Pals - This program is recommended for boys
      in housing projects between five and eighteen years of
      age and adult men who serve as models, friends, and
      teachers. Youth pals are to be obtained by organizations
      who sponsor the Pals for Manhood Program. By knocking
      on doors and visiting courtyards in housing developments,
      between 10:00 a.m. and 3:45 p.m., in the summer, their
      members can obtain participants.

2.   Adult Pals should be members of the participating
      organizations, other interested citizens, and reformed
      single fathers who reinforce the efforts of the
      organizations. One man should be responsible for only
      one apartment -- all boys, siblings, and relatives, in a
      particular household.

3.   Objective - The objective is to strengthen black manhood.
      That is, set in motion the implementation of a new criteria
      for manhood. This new criteria should focus on love
      for self, love for black women, sex power (abstinence),
      sperm control, a positive self image, education, work
      achievement, quality treatment of black women, warmth,

151

sensitivity, clear and frequent communication about all matters pertaining to them, fluency, character, honesty, and positive courage. As far as black women are concerned, association with black men should always be a nonregrettable experience which can only occur with comparable moral, social, and economic achievements.

4. Organization Procedure - The black ministerial alliance in each city should organize all churches, including those black churches not affiliated with the association. Also, a community group should plan an organizational meeting for other interested groups. A working agenda for both organizational meetings could include: (1) selection of the housing development to be used as a pilot project, (2) location of each organization's households (obtain map from city's housing department), (3) selection of date for progress reports and revision of program agenda and procedures, (4) establishment of assessment and follow up procedures and, (5) selection of program beginning and ending dates.

The representatives should take this information to their individual organizations. A working agenda for these meetings could be: (1) a full report of the general meeting of all participating organizations (groups associated with the ministerial association will give a report from their group while those in the community organizations will present their report), (2) discussion of objectives, agenda, and procedures, (3) organizational endorsement of program, (4) assignment of each adult pal to a specific apartment, in the pilot housing project, and (5) development of procedure for obtaining substitute apartments because a family does not care to participate or there are no children between ages five and eighteen.

Once these details are complete, each church and each comunity organization should sponsor a training workshop for participating men. Along with teaching them how to implement the Pals for Black Manhood Agenda, emphasis should be placed on warmth, congeniality, and friendship between the men and their pals. It should be a buddy relationship that allows the young pals to be on a first name basis with their mentors/buddies and their interaction should occur in the home of the youth pal, unless they occasionally go to a ball game or take the young men to see their homes.

The next step would be to implement the Pals for Black Manhood Agenda. However, upon completion of a reasonable portion of the agenda, individual organizations should meet and assess their progress and determine revisions in the program and procedures. Representation from each umbrella group should pool their findings to make revisions in the agenda and procedures. Subsequently, each of the umbrella organizations -- ministerial association, and community organizations -- should hold a general meeting and repeat the assessment procedures and, as far as possible, decide a common set of revisions.

Pals for Black Manhood Agenda: A Home Sex Education Program

The course should last eight weeks. Each adult pal should visit his protege once a week. Such visit should include help with young pals' school work as well as human sexuality training. If the program is implemented in the summer, the pals should visit the library weekly, read and discuss books about achievers in all fields of education, the arts, and sports. This program is intended to sharpen the motivation, family, academic, and sexual knowledge of young pals.

I.   The Meaning of Manhood

    A.   Achievement: Education and Employment

    B.   Daily School Preparation

    C.   Honesty

    D.   Character

    E.   Courage

    F.   Discipline

    G.   High Morality

    H.   Optimism

    I.   Self Respect

    J.   Sensitivity (caring)

K. Development of the Ability to Love (deep concern for the welfare of black women)

L. Warm Loving Disposition

M. Dependability

N. Truthfulness

O. Clarity of Speech

P. Skill in Use of Standard English

Q. The Essence of Black Girls/Women

R. Acceptable Ways Young Boys/Men Can Enhance Black Girls' Self Image

S. Constant Practice of All These Traits

T. Strict Adherence to Parental Advice

U. Black Male Sex Power

II. Contraception

A. Types

B. Double Contraception Image

C. Correct Ways to Use Male and Female Contraception

D. Advantages of Contraception

E. Boy-Girl Communication About Use and Advantages

F. Menstruation

G. Conception

H. Reasons for Avoiding Impregnating Girls

I. Self Image that Precludes Unmarried Fatherhood

III.   Experiences of Young Men who Become Single Fathers

A.   Nature of Fatherhood

1.   Time consuming
2.   Heavy Financial Responsibility
3.   Deprivation of personal freedom
4.   Unfaithfulness of mothers of children
5.   Personal unfaithfulness
6.   Preference for girls who don't have children
7.   Family interference
8.   Adult status but yet a child
9.   Economic insufficiency
10.   Difficult relations with mother of child
11.   Damage to emotions of best friend (mother)

B.   Reactions to News of Its Onset

1.   Shock and Disturbance
2.   Mixed Emotions

C.   Economic Support

1.   Economic insufficiency
2.   Toddler fatherhood -- near benign neglect of children and mothers of their children (economically and emotionally)

D.   Effect on Love Relationship

1.   In general, pregnancy or child birth usually destroys love between a man and his girlfriend
2.   Men prefer girls who do not become pregnant and bear children outside marriage

E.   Behavior to Avoid

1.   Self image based on distortion of girl's previously beautiful body
2.   Desire for a child outside marriage
3.   Early marriage
4.   Quiet girls
5.   Girls who desire motherhood outside marriage
6.   Girls who dislike condoms

F.   The Feelings of Single Fathers -- Instead of Father-
      hood

      1.   They prefer a good education and job
      2.   Would like to be better off financially
      3.   Wish they either had put women aside or
            used birth control
      4.   Wish they had dedicated themselves to one
            girl

IV.   The Responsibilities of a Man Who Impregnates a Girl

V.   We suggest this program also include the Dating / Courting
      For Success Unit recommended for the Human Sexuality
      Training in Schools: Seventh Through Twelfth Grade
      Model

VI.   Culminating Activity

      The churches and community organizations could hold
      a joint day's conference with the adult and youth pals
      and their parents. The agenda could include a review
      of information all boys have been convinced to follow
      and certificates for commitment to avoidance of single
      parenthood.

      Following the eight week course, each adult pal should
      visit his pal one hour three times a month until the pal
      reches eighteen. An adult pal who discontinues his role
      should be replaced immediately by a well prepared
      substitute.

BIBLIOGRAPHY

Banks, Ann. First Person American. New York: Vintage Books, 1980.

Barnes, Annie S. "The Black Beauty Parlor Complex in A Southern City." Phylon 36, 1975, 149-154.

Barnes, Annie S. "The Black Kinship System." Phylon XLII, 1981, pp. 369-380.

Barnes, Annie S. The Black Middle Class Family. Bristol: Wyndham Hall Press, 1985.

Barnes, Annie S. Black Women: Interpersonal Relations in Profile. Bristol: Wyndham Hall Press, 1986.

Bernard, Jessie. Marriage and Family Among Negroes. Englewood Cliff: Prentice Hall, Inc., 1966.

Broderick, Carlfred B. "Social Heterosexual Development Among Urban Negroes and Whites." Journal of Marriage and The Family. 27, 1965, pp. 200-203.

Carmon, Naomi. "Poverty and Crime." Sociological Perspectives 28, 1985, 403-417.

Clark, Kenneth B. Dark Ghetto. New York: Harper & Row, Publishers, 1965.

Cox, Frank D. American Marriage: A Changing Scene. Dubuque: William C. Brown, 1972.

Dash, Leon. "At Risk: Chronicles of Teen-Age Pregnancy," The Washington Post, 26-31 January 1986, Reprint, pp. 1-28.

Drake, St. Clair and Horace R. Cayton. Black Metropolis, Vol. II. New York: Harper & Row Publishers, 1945.

Edelstein, Rosalind I. "In the Poverty Cycle," Social Casework 53, 1972, pp. 418-424.

Ferrarotti, Franco. "The Poor of New York" Part I, La Critica Sociologica 23, (Abstract), 1972, pp. 184-190.

Frazier, E. Franklin. The Negro Family in the United States. Chicago: The University of Chicago Press, 1957.

Gans, Herbert J. "The Positive Functions of Poverty," American Journal of Sociology 78, 1972, pp. 275-289.

Garland, Patricia. "Teenage Illegitimacy in Urban Ghettos" in Unmarried Parenthood. New York: National Council on Illegitimacy, 1967, pp. 24-39.

Glazer, Nathan and Daniel Patrick Moynihan. Beyond the Melting Pot. Cambridge: The M.I.T. Press and Harvard University Press, 1963.

Goode, William J. "Illegitimacy in the Caribbean Social Structure" American Sociological Review, 25, 1960, pp. 21-30.

Goode, William J. "Illegitimacy, Anomie, and Cultural Penetration" American Sociological Review, 26, 1961, pp. 910-925.

Griswold, Barbara B. and Kermit T. Wiltse, and Robert W. Roberts. "Illegitimacy Recidivism Among AFDC Clients." In Unmarried Parenthood. National Council on Illegitimacy, New York, 1967, pp. 7-23.

Haney, C. Allen et al. "Some Consequences of Illegitimacy in A Sample of Black Women" Journal of Marriage and the Family, 37, 1975, pp. 359-366.

Hannerz, Ulf. Soulside. New York: Columbia University Press, 1969.

Harrington, Michael. The Other America. New York: The MacMillian Co., 1962.

Harrington, Michael. "Rediscovering the Other Americans: Michael Harrington's Contribution." In David J. Rothman and Sheilia M. Rothman (Eds.) On Their Own. Reading: Addison-Wesley Publishing Company, 1972, pp. 203-209.

Hendricks, Leo E. "Black Unwed Adolescent Fathers." In Lawrence E. Gary (Ed.) Black Men. Beverly Hills: Sage Publications, 1981, pp. 131-138.

Hill, Robert B. The Strengths of Black Families. New York: Emerson Hall Publishers, 1971.

Himes, Joseph S. "Some Reactions To A Hypothetical Premarital Pregnancy of 100 Negro College Women." Marriage and Family Living. 3, 1964, pp. 344-347.

Irelan, Lola M. et al. "Ethnicity, Poverty, and Selected Attitudes: A Test of the "Culture of Poverty Hypothesis." Social Forces 47, 1969, 405-413.

Kerbo, Harold R. "The Stigma of Welfare and a Passive Poor," Sociology and Social Research 60, (Abstract), 1976, pp. 173-187.

Kutner, Nancy G. "The Poor vs. the Non-Poor: An Ethnic and Metropolitan-Nonmetropolitan Comparison." The Sociological Quarterly 16, 1975, pp. 250-263.

Kutner, Nancy G. and Shirley S. Weeks. "The Relation of Ethnicity, Poverty, and Local Tradition to Family Structure and Attitudes in Honolulu." Urban Anthropology 6, 1977, 329-343.

Leacock, Eleanor Burke. The Culture of Poverty. New York: Simon and Schuster, 1971.

Lewis, Hylan. Blackways of Kent. New Haven: College and University Press, 1955.

Lewis, Hylan. (Cf. "Intergenerational Poverty, Charles Willie) Child Rearing Among Low Income Families Washington: Washington Center for Metropolitan Studies, 1961, pp. 10-11.

Lewis, Hylan. "Agenda Paper No. V: The Family: Resources for Change-Planning Sessoin for the White House Conference "To Fulfill These Rights." In Lee Rainwater and William L. Yancey (Eds.) The Moynihan Report and the Politics of Controversy, 1967, pp. 314-343.

Lewis, Oscar. Five Families. New York: John Wiley & Sons, Inc., 1959.

Lewis, Oscar. The Children of Sanchez. New York: Random House, 1961.

Lewis, Oscar. La Vida. New York: Random House, 1965.

Liebow, Elliot, Tally's Corner. Boston: Little, Brown and Company, 1967.

Light, Ivan and Charles Choy Wong. "Protest or Work: Dilemmas of the Tourist Industry in Ameican Chinatowns." American Journal of Sociology 80, 1975, 1342-1368.

Malinowski, Bronislaw. "Parenthood-The Basis of Social Structure." In Robert W. Roberts (Ed.) The Unwed Mother New York: Harper & Row Publishers, 1966, pp. 25-41.

Martin, Elmer P. and Joanne Mitchell Martin. The Black Extended Family. Chicago: University of Chicago Press, 1978.

Mogull, Robert G. "American Poverty in the 1960's." Phylon 33, 1972, pp. 161-168.

Moynihan, Daniel P. "The Negro American Family." In Lee Rainwater and William L. Yancey (Eds.) The Moynihan Report and the Politics of Controversy. Cambridge: The M.I.T. Press, 1967 pp. 5-14.

Moynihan, Daniel P. "The Tangle of Pathology." In Lee Rainwater and William L. Yancey (Eds.) The Moynihan Report and the Politics of Controversy. Cambridge: The M.I.T. Press 1967, pp. 29-45.

Moynihan, Daniel P. "The Roots of the Problem." In Lee Rainwater and William L. Yancey (Eds.) The Moynihan Report and the Politics of Controversy. Cambridge: The M.I.T. Press 1967, pp. 15-27.

160

Norfolk Planning Commission. Taylor-Murphy Institute Census Data Analysis, University of Virginia, Charlottesville, 1980 & 1984.

Norfolk Redevelopment and Housing Authority. Young Park-Va 6-10; Calvert Park Va 6-11, Norfolk, Virginia, 1986.

Oyemade, Ura Jean. "The Rationale for Head Start As A Vehicle for the Upward Mobility of Minority Families: A Minority Perspective." American Orthopsychiatric Association 55, 1985, 591-602.

Pope, Hallowell. "Unwed Mothers and Their Sex Patterns." Journal of Marriage and The Family. 29, 1967, pp. 187-193.

Rainwater, Lee. "The Gift of Self: A Lower Class Adaptation." In James E. McKeown and Frederick T. Tietze (Eds.) The Changing Metropolis. Boston: Houghton Mifflin Co., 1971, pp. 23-27.

Reiss, Ira L. "Premarital Sexual Permissiveness Among Negroes and Whites." American Sociological Review. 29, 1964, pp. 688-698.

Roebuck, Julian and Marshal L. McGee. "Attitudes Toward Premarital Sex and Sexual Behavior Among Black High School Girls. Journal of Sex Research. vol. 13, May 1957, 104-114.

Rubinstein, Robert A. "Reciprocity and Resource Deprivation Among the Urban Poor in Mexico City." Urban Anthropology 4, 1975, pp. 251-264.

Rutledge, Aaron L. and Gertrude Zemon Gass. Nineteen Negro Men. San Francisco: Jossey-Bass, Inc. 1968.

Ryan, William. Blaming the Victim. New York: Vintage Books, 1971.

Schulz, David A. Coming Up Black. Englewood Cliff: Prentice-Hall, Inc. 1969.

Schulz, David A. "The Role of the Boyfriend in Lower-Class Negro Life." In Charles v. Willie (Ed.) The Family Life of Black People. Columbus: Charles E. Merrill Publishing Company, 1970, pp. 231-243.

Shimkin, Demitri B. et al. "The Black Extended Family: A Basic Rural Institution and A Mechanism of Urban Adaptation." In Demitri B. Shimkin et al. (Eds.) The Extended Family in Black Soceities." The Hague: Mouton Publishers, 1978, pp. 25-147.

Stack, Carol B. All Our Kin. New York: Harper & Row, Publishers, 1974.

Stokes, Carl B. "The Poor Need Not Always Be With Us." Social Science Quarterly, 51, 1971, pp. 821-826.

Valentine, Charles A. Culture and Poverty. Chicago: The University of Chicago Press, 1968.

Virginia Vital Statistics Annual Report. Richmond: Center for Health Statistics, 1980-84.

Willie, Charles V. "Intergenerational Poverty." In The Family Life of Black People. Columbus: Charles E. Merrill Publishing Co., 1970, pp. 316-330.

Willie, Charles. A New Look at Black Families. Bayside: General Hall, Inc., 1976.

Winebrenner, Lawrence M. Basic Facts on Poverty. Homewood: Learning Systems Company, 1974.